The Herball's GUIDE TO
BOTANICAL
DRINKS

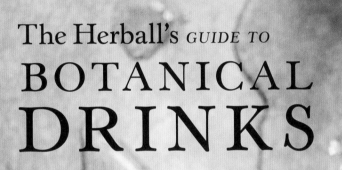

The Herball's GUIDE TO
BOTANICAL
DRINKS

Using *the* alchemy *of* plants *to* create
potions *to* cleanse, restore, relax *&* revive

Michael Isted

jacqui
small

DEDICATION
This book is dedicated to the plants.

Design, layout and photography
© 2017 Quarto Publishing Group plc
Text copyright © 2017 Michael Isted

First published in 2018 by
Jacqui Small
an imprint of The Quarto Group
The Old Brewery
6 Blundell Street
London N7 9BH
United Kingdom
T (0)20 7700 6700 **F** (0)20 7700 8066

Publisher: Jacqui Small
Senior Commissioning Editor: Fritha Saunders
Managing Editor: Emma Heyworth-Dunn
Designer and Art Director: Rachel Cross
Editor: Lucy Bannell
Photography: Susan Bell
Production: Maeve Healy

ISBN: 978 184780 927 8

A catalogue record for this book is available
from the British Library.

2020 2019 2018
10 9 8 7 6 5 4 3 2 1

Printed in China

Botanical illustrations: *cleavers (p.18) Foxyliam/
Shutterstock; hawthorne (p.21) Mamita/Shutterstock;
lemon balm (p.21) Mamita/Shutterstock; chamomile
(p.27) Hein Nouwens/Shutterstock; damiana (p.27)
Foxyliam/Shutterstock; ground ivy (p.20); passion flower
(p.28); coriander (p.32) Wellcome Library, London.
Wellcome Images.* Illustration: *sun and moon (p.13)
Lestyan/Shutterstock*

Quarto is the authority on a wide range of topics.
Quarto educates, entertains and enriches the lives of
our readers – enthusiasts and lovers of hands-on living.
www.QuartoKnows.com

Contents

INTRODUCTION

This book is a celebration of plants, a contemporary collection of recipes designed to help you engage with the nature that surrounds you. With the help of the plants, I will show you new and exciting ways in which you can create delicious, magical, alchemical preparations.

The drinking of plants is central to enhancing our health, both directly and indirectly. It helps us feel connected to our immediate environment and the universe, it offers us grounding and a purpose in life.

In every part of life, whether in your kitchen, local shops, or the bars and fashion world in which I spend much of my time – even in packaging – the botanical influence is there for all to see. Everything is made from plants, whether it's vermouth, toothpaste, perfume, tea, or the drugs that we rely upon. Even the term 'drug' used to mean 'dried herb'.

As a herbalist, I am committed to creating dynamic ways to use herbs, by engaging with nature, sharing rituals that can help us all to connect with the plants. Whether it is by distilling sage from the garden, picking rosemary to make a fresh infusion, or eating blackcurrants straight from the bush, there are so many ways we can get more in tune with the plants that surround us, to enrich our lives and instil a sense of purpose.

I want to bring some excitement to the world of herbal medicine, to drinks and to you. I draw inspiration from looking back through history at the ancient alchemical preparations of our ancestors, and the incredible ways in which herbal remedies were created and administered. Many of these ancient methods and formulas are more exciting than some that are commonly used today, so, in this book, I would like to shed new light on some of those old ways; open a portal through which to reintroduce and reinvigorate these ancient recipes.

Having worked in the food and drink industry for my whole life, creating drinks for hotels, restaurants, bars and spas all over the world, I was happy… but I knew there was something more to come. I decided to give up my job and dedicate my time to learning from the plants and from other people who had spent their lives doing the same. Once I took that step and studied nutrition and herbal medicine, spending more of my time with the plants, everything started to make sense. The plants gave me purpose. I understood more about myself and about life. I'm still on that journey, trying to figure it all out, but the plants are certainly guiding me down a vibrant, exciting and colourful pathway.

We have co-evolved with these brilliant, dynamic organisms that support our life on this planet. They are the food that we eat, they create the air that we breathe, they give us everything, even down to the simple pleasure of a bunch of flowers on the table. We are nothing without plants, trees and fungi. Yet we have treated nature with disdain and disrespect: polluting the air, the waters, the meadows; we've bred and genetically modified plants, messed around with their genes for our own (supposed) gains; and treated them like a commodity. We have to show more respect to nature and reframe the narrative. As the great spiritual leader Sri Mata Amritanandamayi says, 'It is not us who protect nature, it is Nature who protects us.'

THE PLANTS

In this section, I aim to give you a very brief history of some of my major influences, introduce you to some of my favourite plants, and start your journey into the ways in which we can process and use herbs in drinks and potions.

A BRIEF HISTORY...

Flowering and non-flowering plants emerged and began to evolve 60 million years ago, producing chemicals (that we call secondary plant metabolites) as defence against herbivores and infections. As we evolved along with these plants, we began to experiment with them, by eating them, or drinking infusions of them: the first herbal teas. We found we could use their compounds to benefit our health, too.

This use of plants for health and pleasure predates written history. All ancient cultures have records of drinking plant potions, whether it's a warm infusion of mint, a sacred blend of ceremonial herbs, or a cup of tea. One of the oldest dates from China in 7,000–6,600 BC. It was a drink prepared from fermented rice, honey, hawthorn berries and grapes, which was kept preserved in pottery jars.

China

The Chinese system of medicine is based around the use of plants and built on thousands of years of experience.

One of the oldest known texts on the use of herbs was written by Emperor Shen Nung around 2,700 BC, documenting the actions of more than 350 herbs on himself. It contained recipes for more than 100 'drinking medicines', some of which are still used today.

Shen Nung assigned the herbs in each of these compounds to different anthropomorphized characters:

~

THE EMPEROR: *the main herb, the boss.*
THE PREMIER: *the herb that 'advises' the Emperor.*
THE ASSISTANT: *the herb that helps the Emperor do its job.*
THE GUIDE: *the herb that prepares the way for the Emperor.*

~

I am influenced by this way of working. I often build a potion around a 'hero' plant that acts like the 'Emperor', asking myself: what does it taste like, how does it smell, what are its actions, and how can I complement those with other plants and flavours?

About 100 years later, Emperor Huang Ti wrote the *Huang Ti Nei Ching (Yellow Classic of Medicine)*, in which he argues that health is based on two basic forces – yin and yang – and influenced by the five elements – water, fire, earth, metal and wood – all of which affect different organs of the body. Herbal formulas were created to support the diet and prevent disease.

During the Han Dynasty, 206 BC–220 AD, the study of herbs was developed further. One of ancient China's most famous doctors – Chang Chung-ching – developed more than 113 compounds and recipes, including the classic formula for cinnamon twig tea, which is still enjoyed today. Working on Shen Nung's formula, it goes like this:

~

THE EMPEROR: *cinnamon, increases blood circulation.*
THE PREMIER: *pai cao, controls temperature.*
THE ASSISTANT: *ginger, calms digestion.*
THE GUIDES: *date and liquorice as vehicle and flavour.*

~

Fast-forward a thousand years or so to the Ming Dynasty, 1,368 AD–1,643 AD, and Shi Lih-tsai. He compounded new herbal formulas, combining eating the right types of food with ingesting and drinking 'tonic' herbs, to strengthen the system.

In 1977, Zhong Yao Da Ci Dian wrote the most comprehensive book on Chinese medicine ever. The basis for many Chinese herbal preparations are there in the form of drinking medicines, boiled for 20–40 minutes and drunk as a decoction (see page 53).

Opposite page: the best herbal drinks are still made in the ancient ways (see Recipes, pages 65–188)

India

Another huge inspiration for me is the ancient Indian system of Ayurveda (*ayur* 'life' and *veda* 'knowledge'), that is around 5,000 years old. Its origins are uncertain and steeped in mythology. It is thought that the name comes from sacred philosophical books called the *Vedas*. Ayurveda developed from these. I'm particularly interested in the fourth book, the *Atharvaveda*, which referenced plants thought to help to cure disease.

The seminal work of two people – Charaka the Physician and Sushruta the Surgeon – who wrote ancient Ayurvedic texts, further detailed the etiology of diseases and which plants could be used to treat them, recording more than 700 plants and formulas, many of which were to be drunk.

Ayurveda is based on the system of the three *doshas* (which express the physical, emotional and mental characteristics of a person). An imbalance of these *doshas* – *kapha*, *vaata* and *pitta* – can result in disease, and would be treated with lifestyle changes, diet and – of course – plant preparations.

The influence of traditional Indian medicine and herbs is prevalent around the world today, with the ubiquitous use of spices such as black pepper or cardamom, and more exotic plants such as *ashwagandha* or *shatavari* becoming increasingly popular for health and pleasure. Many of the potions in this book are inspired by Ayurveda and feature Indian herbs.

Egypt

The oldest Sumerian medical tablet of the third millennium lists the use of plants such as thyme, myrtle and tree resins, all of which I'm sure would have been taken as some form of drink. In ancient Egypt, The Pyramid Texts of 3,000 BC – one of the oldest sacred texts – included plant preparations and the first *kyphi* (a compound incense formula).

The Ebers Papyrus, a 110-page scroll, dates to about 1,550 BC, and is the oldest medical document of ancient Egypt. It contains more than 700 plant formulas, including some for frankincense, cinnamon and mastic gum.

Greece

The great Greek healer, Hippocrates (460 BC), is known as the father of modern medicine. *The Hippocratic Corpus*, believed to be a compilation of his work, features more than 130 medicinal substances, most of which are herbs, such as barley, nettle, fennel and pennyroyal.

The earliest surviving Greek herbal is called the *Historia Plantarum* or 'Enquiry into Plants', collated by plant biologist Theoprastus (371–287 BC). It was one of the first texts that detailed how to administer herbs and noted their nutritional and health benefits.

Mithridates VI, King Of Pontus (135 BC), is an extremely influential figure in the roots of plant-based potions. He was obsessed with poisons and antidotes, as his father was poisoned by his mother… and poisoning was all the rage back then.

Mithridates teamed up with a brilliant botanist, physician and skilled pharmacologist called Crataeus. They forged a strong bond, and became an early dream team of phytotherapy (herbal medicine), whipping up cocktails of herbs, creating exceptionally powerful potions. They used micro-doses of poison to protect themselves from poisoning, experimenting with gentian and deadly nightshade (and even vipers). It is believed that Crataeus may have been the first scholar to use illustrations of herbs drawn from the plants themselves.

One of Mithridates's and Crataeus's most famous potions was the 'mithridatum', a combination of herbs from Egypt. It included some of the plants from traditional *kyphi* incense mixtures: cassia, cinnamon, myrrh and oil of balanos (from the *Balanites aegyptiaca* tree, native to North Africa).

The mithridatum was developed over the years. Galen of Pergamum, 131–200 AD, a prominent Greek physician, developed Theriac 64, a drug containing 64 different herb preparations, based on the mithridatum. You can find my more streamlined contemporary version of the mithridatum on page 158.

Arabia and Persia

The Arabs and Persians took the knowledge of the Greeks and Egyptians to the next level. Persia and its educational establishments were pivotal in advancing the understanding of the use of plants.

With my love of perfume and ancient Egyptian incense and perfume formulas, I am strongly influenced by the work of Persian and Arabic physicians of the ninth and tenth centuries who developed them. Especially the texts of Al Kindi and Ibn Sina (known as Avicenna), who both advanced distillation techniques.

United Kingdom

My book could not have been written without the work of herbalists a little closer to home, especially the old herbals, created by the likes of John Gerard (1545–1612), and Nicholas Culpeper (1616–1654).

Monasticism & The Monks: In the Middle Ages, the skills of healing, the cultivation of medicinal plants, and the preparation of drugs moved to monasteries. The physician-monks grew sage, anise, mint, sage, savory and tansy, not only to prepare medicines, but to make potions for pleasure, creating herbal beers, meads and wines, many of which are either still available, or have at least inspired many modern drinks.

…and Asterix!

I couldn't write about the history of herbalism without a brief nod to the great fictional alchemists in the Asterix books. Getafix, Botanix and Suffix were village druids who created elixirs, including a strength-enhancing magic potion to give them strength to beat the Romans…

We are witnessing a renaissance of plant-based drinks, such as gin, vermouth, herbal aperitifs, digestifs and bitters, all developed from ancient herbal remedies. I always look to the past for inspiration – from the old herbals, recipes from the monasteries, South American shamans, Ayurveda or Arabic texts on distilling – to find new, modern ways to make delicious potions.

Influence of Sun & Moon

Our ancestors would always use the Moon as a guide, working with lunar cycles to understand when to plant, grow, nurture, harvest and process plants. At certain times during the moon cycle, as it does with the tides, the Moon will help to draw out constituents and flavours from plant preparations. As highlighted in biodynamic farming, the position or phase of the Moon has a profound effect on collecting, preparing, distilling, macerating and using plants and preparations, with the full moon often cited as a good time to harvest.

An autumnal new moon is thought to be a great time to harvest roots, as the energy of the plants has descended into the roots. And it is said that leaves of nettle should be collected only when the Moon is on the wane, when a plant's vitality is in the leaves. Flowers should always, where possible, be collected in the warmth of the Sun, with the flowers open, the full vibrancy of the Sun radiating from the blooms… the perfect time to capture their vibrancy and potency.

Just as a plant's growth and decline is influenced by the forces of the Sun and the Moon, we too must work – or try to work – with nature's rhythms, the natural inhalation and exhalation of the seasons, the Sun and the Moon. I always like to leave extracts, tinctures or preparations to inhale and exhale during a full lunar cycle, to let them breathe and extract to their fullest.

I also leave certain preparations outside overnight during a full or new moon with the fresh plants. During spring and summer, I leave certain preparations out to 'charge' and harness the Sun's vibrancy and energy… but more on all of this in the recipe section (see pages 65–188).

THE SEASONS & THE HARVEST

Wherever you are in the world, certain plants – and certain parts of plants – will be available to you at different times of the year.

Here are some general guidelines about harvesting and collecting plants; for further information please refer to each individual plant (see pages 16–39). For details on processing them, see pages 40–62.

Leaves, stems and aerial parts
This is all parts of a plant that grow above ground. Most leaves can be collected throughout the growing season, though many are normally at their most vibrant during spring and early summer. If you are collecting the entire aerial part of the plant, this is usually best done just before – or just as – it is coming into flower.

Always harvest, if possible, on sunny, dry mornings or afternoons, and get permission from the plant first (see page 41).

Flowers
Harvest flowers throughout their blooming period and at different times of the day so as to capture the varying flavours, aromas and constituents throughout the flowering season. For example, flowers from hawthorn or St John's wort have a much better flavour and more active constituents when they are young, before they bloom entirely, and I find they are better harvested in the afternoon sun. But rose is much, much better just as it comes into full bloom and harvested early in the morning. There is not only one way to do this, so use your intuition, get to know the plants and the climate in your part of the world. After spending some time with the plants, you will begin to understand how best to work with them to capture their beauty.

Fruits
Fruits tend to ripen in mid- to late-summer and are ready to harvest from the end of summer into early autumn (fall). The hardier fruits such as rosehips and hawthorn berries will be available late into autumn (fall), even early winter. Softer fruits such as damsons, blackberries and plums need to be collected just before they are fully ripe, unless you are eating or drinking them immediately. Wild strawberries and raspberries are ready to pick during the peak summer months… there is not one size fits all. You will notice that some years the blackberries come early, some years later. Keep a look out for them and tune into the plants, they will let you know when they are ready.

Seeds
Seeds should be collected carefully when they are fully ripened. They might need a little drying, but most of the time this is not necessary; just harvest them on a dry day so they do not get moist.

Roots
Roots tend to be harvested in the autumn (fall) when the aerial parts die back and the energy of spring and summer starts to head back down into the ground. You want as much of the energy of the plant in the root as possible, so let the aerial parts die back and allow the sap to return to the root. The roots of perennial plants (those that live longer than two years) can be dug up very early in spring, immediately before the plant's shoots appear for the season, so you capture the sap and energy of the plant in the root. Generally, perennial plant roots should not be harvested in a plant's first year, they should be given at least two years to develop.

It is quite unusual to harvest the roots of annual plants (those with a life cycle of one year), but, if you are doing so, they should be dug up just before the plant goes into flower.

The influence of the moon is also key when harvesting roots. If possible, roots should be dug up during a new moon, as the lunar gravity pulls the water and energy up, leaving the roots more vibrant and full of energy… and also making it easier for you to harvest them!

THE PLANT GUIDE

On the pages that follow I will introduce you to my favourite plants – those plants to which I return time and again. Almost all of these are used in the drinks recipes in this book, although I've also included some other plants that I love and use in my work. The plants in this guide are all edible, but do bear in mind that not all parts of every plant are edible, so please follow my advice about which part to use and in what quantities. For safety purposes, all plants should be correctly identified before harvesting and using.

From left to right: lime blossom; fennel & motherwort; valerian, yarrow & St John's wort; meadowsweet & chamomile

Spring Herbs

CLEAVERS *Galium aparine*
OTHER NAMES: *goosegrass, sticky willy.*
NATIVE TO: *Europe, North Africa and Asia, now found widely throughout the USA, Canada, Mexico, Central America, South America and Australia.*

As a child, I used to have great fun in spring, sticking this to people's backs whilst exclaiming 'sticky willy'! It's my first memory of this plant.

It has since become my go-to herb for a spring cleanse, and a favourite for juicing (see page 70), picked on a dry morning. It also makes a great cold infusion with water, as it contains many water-soluble constituents.

Cleavers is a fantastic lymphatic cleansing herb, traditionally used as a blood purifier and for a wide range of skin disorders. It is extremely useful for detoxification, with mild diuretic and anti-inflammatory qualities.

Cleavers grows profusely at the very beginning of spring and throughout summer, but the aerial parts of the plant are best picked and juiced before flowering. It can also be drunk as a fresh or dried decoction or infusion, steeped in cold water overnight (see page 49).

Recipes: pages 68, 70, 76

NETTLE *Urtica doica*
OTHER NAMES: *stinging nettle*
NATIVE TO: *Europe, North America, North Africa and parts of Asia; now found in many other parts of the world.*

Nettle was a childhood adversary, as we got stung while playing, but now is a dear friend. The leaves are a storehouse of chlorophyll and folic acid, hence its traditional use as a blood builder, and are crammed full of vitamins and minerals, including vitamin C, vitamin A, iron, silicon and potassium, useful for strengthening the lungs, stomach and organs of detoxification (the bladder, liver and kidneys). The histamine content also makes it good for treating allergies.

Pick the leaf at the beginning of spring before it flowers, choosing the light green tips of a young plant on a dry, sunny morning, wearing gloves, and ensure the stem is not too woody. Should you get stung, there is normally plantain nearby that, rubbed on, relieves the pain. Enjoy in a juice or smoothie (see page 70), as a decoction or tincture, or fresh or dried as an infusion (see pages 53 and 49).

Recipes: pages 68, 70, 76, 78

DANDELION *Taraxacum officinale fol, flos, radix*
OTHER NAMES: *lion's tooth, pis-en-lit*
NATIVE TO: *Europe and Asia; now found widely throughout the USA, southern Africa, New Zealand, Australia and India.*

I love spotting the first rosettes of dandelion, giving birth to a cluster of magical bright yellow florets that open in the spring sunshine. Due to its mere abundance, dandelion is often overlooked, but it is a valuable cleansing herb.

The diuretic leaf and root are ideal for cleansing the kidneys. It is also a cooling bitter, packed with vitamin A, vitamin C, iron, B6, calcium and thiamine, and a great natural source of potassium. Both the leaf and flower have a toning effect on skin, while the root is full of therapeutic glycosides and triterpenoids that help the organs of detoxification.

In the spring, collect the leaf and flower on sunny mornings; collect the root in late summer and early autumn (fall) as a component for bitters (see page 54).

As a juice, the leaf is a useful aperitif, as it is a digestive stimulant. The flowers are less bitter and have a more honeyed taste.

Recipes: pages 69, 70, 78, 150, 162

PLANTAIN *Plantago spp, lanceolata, major, coronopus*
OTHER NAMES: *buck horn, lamb's tongue*
NATIVE TO: *British Isles, and widespread in the Americas and Australia.*

The appearance of these lance-shaped leaves is a reminder that spring is here. Plantain is abundant across the globe and the young, tender leaves are best

Clockwise, from main photograph: plantain; dandelion; cleavers

collected early in spring before it flowers, but can be harvested throughout spring and summer. They are anti-inflammatory and antiseptic, so are great rubbed on stings, cuts or grazes.

Plantain has several antioxidant flavonoids, soothing mucilage and astringent tannins as well as vitamin A, vitamin C, vitamin B6 and potassium.

It is a cooling bitter with an alkalizing action on blood pH and combines well with dandelion leaf to cleanse the bladder, small intestine and gall bladder. Traditionally, plantain is used to treat respiratory problems and for its astringency. I juice the leaves for a cleansing juice or tonic (see page 76). Pick them on a dry, sunny morning, juice as soon as possible and freeze any excess. Plantain makes a superb decoction, or can be dried to create an infusion.

Recipes: pages 76, 80

SWEET VIOLET *Viola odorata*
OTHER NAMES: *garden violet*
NATIVE TO: *Europe and Asia; now found widely in the USA, South America and Australia.*

The heavenly scented, deep-purple blooms of wild violet flower at the end of winter and are normally over by the time spring kicks into action. You must be quick, as they appear overnight and, before you know it, they have gone. Violets produce self-pollinating closed blooms in autumn (fall), but these do not produce the same heavenly scent as those lovely, surprising blossoms of late winter.

I make a simple water infusion to capture the beautiful aromatic qualities. A syrup made from the flowers is traditionally used as a cough remedy. I make a water infusion of violets for its divine taste and calming, almost ethereal effects, and use it in ice cubes to beautiful effect. It's a great simple plant potion with which to welcome in the joys of spring and say goodbye to the winter.

Recipe: page 84

GROUND IVY *Glechoma hederacea*
OTHER NAMES: *haymaids, hedgemaids, creeping Charlie, cat's foot*
NATIVE TO: *Europe and South-west Asia; now found widely in the USA.*

It covers the grassland, fields and roadsides in early spring, its little trumpet-shaped purple flowers and furry leaves are only a few inches from the ground, so it can be difficult to spot. The aerial parts of the plant are best collected early in spring and summer.

It was traditionally used for coughs, other problems associated with the lungs, headaches, and for its diuretic actions. Ground ivy has a very particular taste that somehow reminds me of a Sunday roast dinner (in a good way!). I like it in combination with other spring plants as a simple infusion, or as part of a more creative plant potion.

Recipe: page 76

BIRCH *Betula pendula*
OTHER NAMES: *silver birch*
NATIVE TO: *Northern Europe and parts of Asia, also grows in Southern Europe and the USA.*

Prized for its life-giving properties in many cultures in the Northern hemisphere, it gifts us sweet nectar or sap that can be collected from the trees in early spring. The young leaves and bark can also be collected in late spring and into early summer, to be dried or used fresh as an infusion, for their cleansing and diuretic actions. The bark contains a triterpenoid called betulinic acid, which is used for infectious diseases and enhances immune function.

You will often find that the birch is home to mushrooms, such as the birch polypore and chaga (particularly in Scandinavia and Russia). They live on the birch and form a symbiotic relationship with it, creating a raft of powerful therapeutic constituents, including large amounts of betulinic acid.

Recipe: page 78

HAWTHORN *Crataegus spp*
OTHER NAMES: *may, whitethorn*
NATIVE TO: *Europe; but grows in North Africa, Western Asia and the USA.*

Hawthorn is a plant I associate most with the heart, abundant and beautiful, lining hedgerows across Europe, it presents us with generous gifts throughout the year.

The flowers and leaf should be collected in spring and the berries in late summer and autumn (fall). The flowers, leaves and berries are used traditionally as a tonic for the heart, the berries make a great syrup for sore throats.

The red berries are known as 'pixie pears'. I tend to make hawthorn preparations with all three parts of the plant – leaf, flower and berry – to collect all the constituents and flavours at the optimum times of the year.

I also collect the berries at different parts of the growth cycle for the same reason (see page 41).

Recipes: pages 124, 150, 168

LEMON BALM *Melissa officinalis*
OTHER NAMES: *balm, bee balm or sweet balm*
NATIVE TO: *Southern Europe and Northern Africa; but now cultivated and grown throughout the world.*

Beautiful Melissa, actually a member of the mint family, is always there when you need her, gentle and welcoming.

Her soft, furry, aromatic green leaves are great if you are feeling down and need some emotional support.

The ancient Greeks traditionally used balm for depression and melancholy. I still do today and I'm not alone, it's a favourite herb to drink to relieve frazzled nerves, for a headache or if you are feeling anxious or down. Freshly picked lemon balm, gently bruised by being clapped in the hand and enjoyed as a hot or cold infusion (see page 47), is a beautifully embracing cup of love.

The leaves can be collected in late spring and summer before and during flowering. Lemon balm will

continue to grow into autumn (fall) and even winter if it's not too cold. She'll be there for you if you need her.

Recipes: pages 83, 106, 131

DAISY *Bellis perenis*
OTHER NAMES: *bruisewort*
NATIVE TO: *Europe; and across the world.*

Another plant I feel we take for granted. It is always there in spring, summer and into autumn (fall). If I think back to my childhood, the daisy – along with the buttercup and dandelion – is among my first memories of plants, they were everywhere. The small white-and-yellow flowers bloom early in spring and can be collected to make daisy chains or a variety of plant potions. Used traditionally to treat coughs and bruises, aches and pains.

The little flowers, although not full of flavour, pack a pepper-like quality with good astringency. They make a pleasant hot or cold infusion or decoction on their own, or in conjunction with other herbs.

Recipe: page 96

ELDER *Sambucus nigra*
OTHER NAMES: *sweet elder*
NATIVE TO: *Central Europe.*

The elder and its creamy white and yellow flowers signals the beginning of summer, while the drooping deep, dark purple berries signal the end. The fragrance of its blossoms fills the air in early summer; harvest them as soon as they blossom. I prefer the flowers early in the bloom, before they brown and end up smelling like sweaty socks.

Harvest the berries at the end of summer; I like to pick them early when they are green and again when they ripen, to collect the full diversity of flavours and active constituents during their development. Note: try not to ingest the berries in large quantities, as they can be emetic (make you sick).

Elderflower is one of the most traditional plant potions in Europe, widely used as a cordial. The flowers and berries are used as traditional remedies for colds, flus and to boost immunity.

Above: elderflower (see page 21)

The elder offers a treasure chest of delicious gifts for us throughout the season, to create some fantastic plant potions.

Recipes: pages 80, 150

RED CLOVER *Trifolium pratense*
OTHER NAMES: *meadow clover, wild clover or cow clover*
NATIVE TO: *Europe, North Africa and Western Asia.*

A member of the legume family, it has long been associated with cows that love to graze on the flowers and leaves. Its small purple flowers appear in early spring and continue to flower throughout summer. The flowers and leaves can be collected throughout the growing year, although I'd recommend picking the flowers early before they turn brown.

Red clover is a tricky herb to dry well without the flowers turning brown, so pick it early when the flowers are still fresh and follow the guidelines on page 42. If purchasing dried red clover, check that they are not brown. I have had to send back many a batch due to poor drying techniques.

Red clover is beautifully nourishing as a hot or cold infusion, with a lovely gentle herbaceous sweetness. Nutrient-dense, it helps with blood circulation and it just feels so great for the skin.

Recipe: page 68

Summer Herbs & Flowers

CALENDULA *Calendula officinalis*
OTHER NAMES: *marigold or pot marigold*
NATIVE TO: *southern Europe; now found widely across Europe, the USA and Western Asia.*

Beautiful bright orange calendula flowers bloom late into summer and autumn (fall), and occasionally into winter. It is the flower of the sun and it is mostly the flowers that are used, though the leaf can also be useful. Both flowers and leaves should only be collected in fine weather.

The flowers make an excellent infusion or decoction to be used internally and externally for its anti-inflammatory actions. I love to run a bath infused with fresh or dried flowers of calendula, it is so nourishing for the skin. A water distillation (hydrosol) of the flowers (see page 60), applied externally, is excellent for inflammatory skin disorders. The leaves can be chewed, juiced or eaten in salads, but also make a wonderful infused vinegar and oxymel (see page 59).

Recipes: pages 174, 186

ROSE *Rosa spp.*
NATIVE TO: *the USA, Western Asia.*

What would life be without the rose? It is harvested for its buds and petals in the summer and fruits (rosehips) in autumn (fall). There are thousands of cultivars. When I discuss roses in this book, I mean two of the most aromatic varieties: *Rosa damascena* and *Rosa centifolia*.

Rose is used for perfume and oil, extracted by distillation. Dried flowers and hips are used for food, health supplements and herbal teas. Roses and rose water form an integral part of many religious ceremonies and, as a food, in the Middle East and North Africa (and in my home), it is an integral part of everyday life and is used by the gallon.

Plants begin to flower in April. In warmer climates, harvesting begins in late April, while in Europe it is nearer the end of May. The concentration of perfume and constituents is at its greatest just as the flowers develop into full bloom; they should be gathered before sunrise with calyx attached, to capture maximum oils.

Recipes: pages 83, 98, 100, 102, 114, 124, 167, 168, 171, 172

LAVENDER *Lavendula angustifolia*
OTHER NAMES: *elf leaf*
NATIVE TO: *the Mediterranean, but grows across Europe to Scandinavia, in North America, Africa, Asia, Australia and the Middle East.*

A sturdy, robust perennial that flowers from late spring and throughout summer. Cultivated and harvested mainly for the fragrant flowers, although the leaf is beautiful too, it is a firm favourite of bees.

Harvest the flowers throughout the growing season, to get different aromatic qualities. I love the greener fresh buds for their vibrant, less pungent aroma, but collect both immature and mature flowers to use in combination. I pass the young flowers through a CO_2 extraction unit (see page 62); it fills the home with the most heavenly scent and puts you in a lavender daze. I always sleep so well after working with lavender. The leaf, too, can be collected much earlier in spring before it matures; it has more vibrant flavours and aromas.

Lavender is classically used for its calming and anti-depressant actions. The oil is fantastic to relieve a headache. It is great dried as an infusion, although in small quantities and in combination with other plants, or it can be overpowering.

Recipes: pages 131, 148, 150, 180, 186

BORAGE *Borago officinalis*
OTHER NAMES: *star flower*
NATIVE TO: *the Mediterranean, but cultivated throughout the world.*

Its brilliant blue star-shaped flowers are normally mobbed by bees in the summer. The leaves and flowers can be collected throughout summer; the flowers will bloom late into summer and into early autumn (fall). Normally one of the last flowers I see the bees working on for the year, it yields a delicious, light honey.

The prickly green leaves make for a wonderfully cool and refreshing juice or cold infusion when picked early in summer (see page 106), they have a fresh cucumber-like flavour. The flowers also make a great cold infusion and a good (if somewhat overused) decoration for drinks and dishes.

Recipe: page 106

CALIFORNIAN POPPY
Eschscholzia california
OTHER NAMES: *cup of gold, golden poppy*
NATIVE TO: *North America and Mexico.*

Is there a more magnificent orange colour than that of the Californian Poppy? The flowers and aerial parts can be harvested throughout late spring and summer, and you can buy it dried, but if possible use it fresh, as you want to harness the vibrancy of the astonishing colour.

The sight of that orange is like a brilliant sunbeam shining right on to the heart. The bright orange flowers open and close with the sun, you can sit and watch it happen. It is traditionally used to relieve pain, headaches and as a sleeping aid. I use it for the same purposes. Californian poppy makes for a calming and sedative plant potion and can help to shine a calming and comforting ray of sunshine, a little like a restorative snooze in the late afternoon sun.

Recipes: pages 90, 98

YARROW *Achillea millefolium*
OTHER NAMES: *milfoil, thousand weed and soldier's wound wort*
NATIVE TO: *Asia, Europe and the USA; found widely in Australia, New Zealand and China.*

The name of this plant comes from Achilles, who is said to have treated wounds with yarrow due to its astringent (drying) actions, while *millefolium* means 'thousand leaf', referring to the many segments of the leaves.

Yarrow grows everywhere, so it always seems to be there for you. The brilliant thousand-leaf leaves unravel early in spring, while the white, or sometimes pink and purple, flowers bloom late in spring and then throughout summer.

Harvest the leaves in spring before the flowers, and collect them throughout the year. The flowers are best collected in late spring and early summer.

Both leaf and flower dry well so are excellent dried for infusions (see page 47). At the first sign of a cold or a fever, a hot water infusion of fresh or dried yarrow is one of my first ports of call.

Recipes: pages 70, 126

Clockwise, from top left: borage; Californian poppy; oat straw; yarrow

Clockwise, from top to bottom: chamomile; Roman chamomile

OAT *Avena sativa*
OTHER NAMES: *common oat, groats or oatmeal*
NATIVE TO: *Europe, Asia and Africa.*

A grass that we have cultivated over thousands of years into one of man's best friends, a staple for us and our animals. Often planted in autumn (fall) and harvested in summer, the plants can be harvested for the seeds and the whole plant, or dried to create oat straw, or processed (rolled and crushed) to create oatmeal or flakes.

Oat straw or dried oat is a favourite herb of mine to create a base for warm herbal infusions (see page 180), excellent for nervous dispositions, calming frayed nerves, and also for nourishing the skin.

Recipe: page 180

CHAMOMILE *Matricaria recutita*
OTHER NAMES: *German chamomile*
NATIVE TO: *Southern and Western Europe; now cultivated in Northern Africa (particularly Egypt), North and South America, India, Asia, Australia and New Zealand.*

One of the most popular medicinal and flavouring herbs in the West for its cosmetic and nutritional value.

Chamomile loves to grow on the peripheries of corn fields, so if you're picking from the wild, make sure the field has not been sprayed with chemicals. Chamomile loves the heat. The flowers and leaves can be collected when the flowers appear in summer. Distilled worldwide for its therapeutic oils, it is called 'blue chamomile', as it contains a constituent called chamazulene, which is a brilliant blue colour.

Chamomile has been used medicinally for thousands of years across many different cultures. Its gentle warming and subtle bitter qualities make it a great digestif. As an infusion it helps to de-stress, calm and relieve anxiety. Its honeyed flavours and aromas make it a versatile herb.

Recipes: pages 131, 180, 188

ROMAN CHAMOMILE *Anthemis nobilis*
OTHER NAMES: *manzanilla, ground apple*
NATIVE TO: *Southern and Western Europe.*

My favoured chamomile, it packs a bit more of a punch, with interesting flavours and a fantastic bitter kick. When just picked, it smells of green apples. The fluffy white flowers can be collected in mid to late summer.

The blue-coloured chamazulene compound also present in Roman chamomile (more abundantly I find, although I have had many a discussion on this) will leach out in hot water if left overnight; drunk cold in the morning, it's a wonderful start to the day. When using Roman chamomile, I recommend using lots of heat to extract the flavours and constituents, as they can be stubborn to extract in cooler water.

Recipes: pages 150, 182

DAMIANA *Turnera diffusa*
OTHER NAMES: *Turnera aphrodisiaca*
NATIVE TO: *South and Central America.*

Damiana is known for its aphrodisiac qualities where it is native. Harvested for its leaves, flowers and stems, it is traditionally used as an anti-depressant, mood enhancer and tonic for the nerves.

Damiana is beautifully perfumed and extremely aromatic with a distinct taste and flavour. When used to create plant potions, it needs to be treated with care, as it can be overpowering.

Excellent as a hot infusion or love potion in conjunction with other plants.

Recipes: none, but try in a love potion (see page 165)

MARSHMALLOW *Althaea officinalis*
OTHER NAMES: *mortification root*
NATIVE TO: *Northern and Southern Europe.*

Its roots, flowers and velvety leaves are famed for their mucilaginous qualities. It is an emollient (helps to soften the skin). The leaves and flowers are harvested late in summer, while the roots should be harvested in autumn (fall). Named 'marsh' as the plant likes damp (fall). Named 'marsh' as the plant likes damp marshland areas to grow and flourish.

The original marshmallow confectionery was created by the ancient Egyptians, who used the gelatinous root whipped with honey and exotic spices to form a medicinal candy. It was developed further by the French, who added egg whites and sugar. Sadly, commercial marshmallow no longer contains *Althaea*.

Marshmallow has a delicious taste with a rich, viscous mouthfeel, giving a moistening and cooling effect. The leaves and flowers are great in a cold or hot infusion, while the roots work well in a decoction or tincture.

Recipes: none, but try a cleansing potion (see page 66)

MEADOWSWEET *Filipendula ulmaria*
OTHER NAMES: *Queen of the meadow, meadwort*
NATIVE TO: *Central and Northern Europe.*

Its unmistakable fluffy white balls of cotton wool-like flowers line moist ditches and roadsides, emitting a smell of floral aspirin across the countryside. When you find meadowsweet, it is normally in large swathes. Famed for its salicylic acid content (from which aspirin is made), it is used traditionally for its digestive calming, astringent, anti-inflammatory and mild pain-relieving actions.

While many are fans of elderflower cordial, I'm much more interested in meadowsweet; it has such an interesting, beguiling aroma. The fresh flowers and leaves make for such an intriguing flavour for many a potion. Meadowsweet tends to flower a little later in summer depending on where you are in the world, and the flowers and leaves can be collected when it goes into bloom.

Recipes: none, but try in a digestif (see page 146)

PASSION FLOWER *Passiflora incarnate*
OTHER NAMES: *passion vine, Maypop*
NATIVE TO: *North, Central and South America, but now grows throughout the world.*

If there was ever a plant trying to tell us that there is more to life than meets the eye, it is the passion flower. Its simple green vine-like exterior opens to the sun to reveal an intricate psychedelic multidimensional floral display that I still marvel at. The hollow fruits can be popped.

Traditionally used for its sedative, hypnotic and anti-depressant calming actions, it is known as the plant of dreams, helping people to sleep and to remember their dreams.

The leaves and flowers can be used. The leaves should be collected late in spring and early summer before the flowers bloom; the flowers should be collected on a sunny day in summer.

Recipe: page 185

ST JOHN'S WORT *Hypericum perforatum*
OTHER NAMES: *klamath weed*
NATIVE TO: *Europe, the Mediterranean and Western Asia.*

Long associated with the mood, for good reason, as the drinking of St John's wort has a very uplifting effect. The plant loves the sun and brings the sunshine into our lives with its bright yellow flowers and what they can do to the body.

The flowers come into bloom around St John's Day on 24 June, and this is the best time to harvest it. In mid-summer the woody green stalks produce bright yellow flowers that project their stamens up to the sun. On crushing the flowers, they produce a red colouring. You can infuse the young flowers in oil in the sun and they will turn the oil a lovely shade of red.

The stems, leaves and flowers should be harvested during summer, when the sun is out, and the plant will produce flowers long into summer. As always, I recommend you pick the flowers immediately after blooming, especially if you are going to dry the plant for a herbal infusion, or it can turn brown quickly.

Recipes: none

VALERIAN *Valeriana officinalis*
OTHER NAMES: *vandal root, set well*
NATIVE TO: *Europe and Western Asia, but introduced into the USA where it thrives.*

Valerian carries an unmistakable aroma from the whole plant. It retains this in its preparations, so when you open a bottle of valerian tincture it's still super-pungent, which I love but so many hate. Cats go nuts for it, too.

Opposite: valerian

When you find a patch of fresh valerian there is an unforgettable beautiful pink hue around the plants, emanating from each of the pink and white flowers. In mid-summer you can spot it and smell it a mile off.

Valerian has long been associated with sleep and its sedative actions. It's a relaxing nervine tonic (it relaxes the nerves) and can be used to relieve pain. It is grown and harvested primarily for its roots, which can be taken in early autumn (fall) from plants that are at least two years old.

Recipe: page 188

WORMWOOD *Artemisia absinthum*
OTHER NAMES: *absinthe*
NATIVE TO: *Europe, North Africa and Western Asia; now naturalized in the USA, too.*

A powerful plant, grown and harvested for its leaves and flowers. The greenish-yellow flowers should be collected in late summer, but you can collect the leaves throughout the growing year.

Wormwood should command respect. I've a soft spot for this plant, I'm attracted to the silvery moon-like qualities apparent in its leaves and flowers. Wormwood is associated with the moon and the virgin Greek goddess Artemis, who treated it as a sacred plant.

It is traditionally used for the treatment of parasites and worms, as a digestive stimulant and bitter. The leaves and flowers, when dried, produce a wonderful silver herb that can be used sparingly to add a touch of aromatic bitterness to a herbal infusion or potion.

Recipes: 150, 160, 174

GINKGO *Ginkgo biloba*
OTHER NAMES: *the maidenhair tree*
NATIVE TO: *China; now growing throughout Asia, Europe, Australia and the USA.*

One of the oldest living organisms on the planet, and the oldest herbal remedy; these trees have been here for over two million years, with some living for more than 1,000 years. Its medicinal use has been recorded for thousands of years. It is traditionally used as a circulatory stimulant, cardiovascular tonic, and blood thinner, with beneficial effects for stimulating the brain and improving memory.

The beautiful and unmistakable double-lobed, fan-shaped leaves are best harvested in early to late summer. They are delightful used fresh or dried in a herbal infusion with hot water.

Recipes: pages 138, 140

ANDROGRAPHIS *Andrographis paniculata*
OTHER NAMES: *king of bitters, kalmegh*
NATIVE TO: *India and Sri Lanka, but widely distributed throughout Asia.*

Andrographis is an annual herb. Historically, in Siddha and Ayurvedic systems, inflammatory respiratory symptoms such as sinusitis and epidemics of influenza were treated with andrographis. It is still widely used for the treatment of respiratory tract infections in India, China, Malaysia and Thailand, and – in conjunction with Siberian ginseng – in Scandinavia, to treat common colds and flu. The aerial parts of the plant are typically used for traditional medicine, particularly the leaves, although the root and whole plant can be used.

As its name suggests, andrographis helps to form an integral part of many traditional 'bitter' formulations.

Recipe: page 152

GOTU KOLA *Centella asiatic*
OTHER NAMES: *Indian pennywort*
NATIVE TO: *India, Asia and the South Pacific.*

Used in Ayurvedic and Chinese medicine for thousands of years as a miracle elixir of life. It is found growing near water in subtropical climates in India, Sri Lanka, South Africa and the South Pacific.

The small fan-shaped green leaves and whitish-pink flowers are harvested in summer. They are traditionally used in Ayurveda for their blood purifying and circulatory stimulating properties, for enhancing memory, revitalizing brain cells and promoting longevity. I like to use gotu kola for any preparations to boost the brain. It is truly wonderful.

Recipe: page 140

Above: ginkgo

Classic Kitchen Herbs

ROSEMARY *Rosmarinus officinalis*
OTHER NAMES: *dew of the sea*
NATIVE TO: *the Mediterranean.*

A go-to herb, rosemary loves the coasts and the sea, but grows everywhere. Wherever I travel there is a rosemary bush close by… nature has a way of subtly hinting.

Rosemary is exceptional because you can pretty much work with it all year round. The leaves and aerial parts can be harvested throughout the year, but are best in spring and summer when the warmth releases larger quantities of flavoursome aromatic oils in the leaves.

It's one of those plants that always seems to be in flower, blooming early in spring all through summer, then again in autumn (fall) and winter.

Packed full of aromatic oils, the leaves and flowers can be harvested and used in the kitchen. There is a potion dedicated to rosemary on page 142. It is also great picked fresh and drunk as a hot infusion if you need a pick-me-up.

Recipes: pages 83, 92, 138, 142

THYME *Thymus vulgaris*
OTHER NAMES: *mother of thyme*
NATIVE TO: *Southern Europe and the Mediterranean.*

Another aromatic beauty, prolific, and used for respiratory issues. It is drunk fresh or dried as an infusion, or used as an infused oil rubbed on the chest. It is packed full of antibacterial oils.

Like many aromatic plants, although thyme grows across the world, both wild and domesticated, it likes the sunshine and heat of the Mediterranean, where those pungent antibacterial, flavoursome oils can develop in the peripheries of the plant.

Thyme flowers in early summer and throughout the summer months; the leaves and aerial parts can be harvested and worked with throughout this time. It tends to get a little woody later in the year and as it matures, but the leaves can still be used.

Recipes: pages 92, 174

CORIANDER *Coriandrum sativum*
OTHER NAMES: *cilantro*
NATIVE TO: *Southern Europe and North Africa, but now cultivated around the world.*

Eponymous with Indian and Central and South American cuisine, it is cultivated for the aerial parts (leaves and flowers) and seeds.

The leaves can be harvested throughout spring and summer and the seeds collected late in summer into autumn (fall); the seeds are dried, or extracted for their volatile oil.

Coriander (cilantro) is a beautifully fragrant plant that people tend to love or hate. I'm a fan and love the distinctive flavour profile that both the leaf and seed can bring to a potion.

Drinking both the leaf and seed is great for stimulating digestive juices, so coriander (cilantro) makes an excellent ingredient for aperitif or digestif potions (see page 146).

Recipes: none, but try in a digestif (see page 146)

TARRAGON *Artemisia dracunculus*
OTHER NAMES: *little dragon*
NATIVE TO: *Southern Europe.*

There are two common types: French and Russian; the French variety is what I am discussing here. (The Russian variety is much less fragrant and lacks the same beautiful flavour.)

One of my favourite culinary herbs because of its beautiful green, fragrant anise-like quality. It's so beautiful, I love to create drinks with tarragon.

The leaves can be collected throughout the summer, it flowers late into summer and the flowers can be used, too. Although you can use dried tarragon, this loses the better part of its aromatic qualities, so this is a herb that is much better fresh. It is also wonderful as a fresh juice or infused in a vinegar or oxymel (see page 59).

Although you do not see it much, a fresh water distillation (hydrosol, see page 60) of tarragon works well; it extracts the aromatic qualities of the plant: highly recommended.

Recipe: page 144

CUCUMBER *Cucumis sativa*
OTHER NAMES: *cowcumber*
NATIVE TO: *Southern Asia, specifically India, but now grown all over the world.*

Known for its bitter qualities in the past, the commercial cucumber has been bred into a plant containing lots of water and little flavour, with much of what remains coming from the seeds and skin. The fruits are harvested in summer, shortly after the first female flowers have opened.

The juice of cucumber is fantastic for its cooling, refreshing qualities, excellent for preparing summer plant potions.

Recipes: pages 90, 106

 GARLIC *Allium sativum*
OTHER NAMES: *stinkweed*
NATIVE TO: *probably central Asia.*

Part of the onion or allium family, this might be the most useful herb available to us. I couldn't live without it. The ancient world loved garlic, particularly the Egyptians, whose use of garlic is recorded in one of the oldest surviving medical texts, the Ebers Papyrus. The Greeks called Egyptians 'the stinking ones', due to the amount of garlic they consumed.

Garlic has a diverse array of usages, both culinary and medicinal, and powerful therapeutic qualities in the kitchen. Its antibacterial and immune-stimulating properties are well documented. Perhaps garlic, a little like black pepper, is underestimated because of its familiarity.

Garlic bulbs should be harvested in mid to late summer, just as the lower leaves turn brown.

Recipe: page 92

 **WILD GARLIC** *Allium ursinum*
OTHER NAMES: *ramson*
NATIVE TO: *Northern Europe, parts of the USA, Asia.*

In early springtime the countryside and woodlands are filled with the sweet smell of wild garlic. The leaves and flowers can be collected in early spring, both before and during flowering, eaten or juiced fresh they are delicious. The seeds are also delicious fresh, or pickled in vinegar; they can be harvested as they develop later in summer.

Recipes: none, but try in recipe on page 92

 FENNEL *Foeniculum vulgare*
OTHER NAMES: *sweet or wild fennel*
NATIVE TO: *the Mediterranean, but grown throughout the world.*

Grown for the bulbs, green tops and seeds, the bulbs can be harvested once they have matured in mid-summer, the tops can be collected throughout the growing season (spring to end of summer), while the seeds should be collected at the end of summer into early autumn (fall).

Fennel is one of my favourite plants for digestion and for its flavour; I use it a great deal for plant potions. The fresh green seeds that form on beautiful umbels (like plant umbrellas) are packed with flavoursome aromatic oils that help to stimulate and settle digestion. Both the bulbs and tops make a cleansing, stomach-settling juice.

Recipes: 68, 70, 88, 90, 92, 115, 142, 144, 150, 154

 SAGE *Salvia officinalis*
OTHER NAMES: *common sage or garden sage*
NATIVE TO: *the Mediterranean.*

What would we do without sage? Salvia is derived from the Latin *salvere* meaning 'to be saved', and sage has saved me on many occasions. As much as I love the sage that grows in my garden, you cannot beat sage from the Mediterranean islands such as Crete or Greece; the heat helps to produce a phenomenal pungent, aromatic feral-

Above: burdock root

like quality in the sage that I oh-so-love.

The leaves can be collected throughout spring and summer, even into autumn (fall) and winter, but are best picked in the height of summer, when those wonderful oils are at their best. The flowers can be harvested late in summer.

Sage's volatile oils are marvellous for soothing sore throats, coughs and colds. The wonderful pungent flavours mean that you can create some delicious potions with sage.

Recipes: pages 83, 88, 92, 104, 160

PARSLEY *Petroselinum crispum*
OTHER NAMES: *devil's oatmeal, petersilie*
NATIVE TO: *the Mediterranean and Northern Africa.*

One of the most widely used culinary herbs, grown and harvested for its aromatic leaves, roots and seeds. The leaves can be collected throughout the growing season, the seeds at the end of summer and the root in the autumn (fall) of the second year of the plant's growth.

Parsley leaves and root make for a brilliant nutrient-dense fresh juice packed with vitamin C, an excellent diuretic and kidney-cleansing herb. It is also useful for cleansing the organs of digestion, particularly the liver. The seeds contain large amounts of volatile oil and are excellent for settling digestion and easing digestive cramps or wind.

Recipes: pages 76, 148, 158

PEPPERMINT *Mentha piperita*
OTHER NAMES: *brandy mint*
NATIVE TO: *North Africa and the Mediterranean.*

It is thought that peppermint is a hybrid of spearmint and water mint.

An extremely popular herb across Europe for its easy refreshing taste when drunk as a herbal infusion, and for its gentle and relaxing effect on the digestive system. Peppermint is also a useful herb for relieving fevers, because it has a diaphoretic action (which means it makes you sweat).

Peppermint is cultivated for its highly aromatic leaves packed full of fragrant oils, which can be collected from late spring into late summer and autumn (fall). Domesticated potted mint can grow abundantly throughout the year indoors and the leaves can be collected all year round.

The fresh or dried leaves make for a great hot or cold infusion; the fresh leaves can also be added to many cold drinks to give a refreshing, cooling quality.

Recipes: pages 76, 88

Autumn (Fall) & Winter Harvest

BURDOCK *Arctium lappa*
OTHER NAMES: *thorny burr, love leaves*
NATIVE TO: *found widely throughout the world.*

I'm a fan of the heart-shaped leaves of burdock, though many people find it a pain due to its size, thorny burrs, ability to multiply and the depth the roots like to travel: 60–90cm (2–3ft), making it hard to remove or harvest.

Burdock is biennial (with a two-year life cycle) and the roots are best harvested (good luck) in its first year during late summer or early autumn (fall), or spring of the second year. Collect the leaves in summer in the first or second year; seeds should be harvested when ripe in the autumn (fall) of the second year.

The fresh root is delicious in salads or as a juice and tastes nothing like the fizzy drink (soda) dandelion and burdock. Due to the challenges of harvesting it, I use dried root (see page 190), or find cultivated fresh roots in Asian stores.

I use it for its cleansing actions, it is fantastic for skin disorders and for the organs of detoxification, particularly the liver.

Recipes: pages 68, 69, 150, 162

JUNIPER *Juniperus communis*
OTHER NAMES: *genever, gin berry*
NATIVE TO: *Central and Northern Europe, but now grows across temperate regions of Europe, Asia, North Africa and North America.*

Famous as a flavouring for gin. However, it is traditionally used for its kidney-cleansing, anti-fungal and antibacterial properties, due to the large amount of volatile oils found in the berries. Berries can be collected late in summer into autumn (fall); leaves can be collected throughout summer.

Recipes: pages 160, 166

Spices, Roots, Resins & Barks

TURMERIC *Curcuma longa*
OTHER NAMES: *haldi, manjal*
NATIVE TO: *India and Southern Asia.*

The golden spice. The name 'turmeric' comes from the Latin *terra merita* (meritorious earth), referring to the bright yellow or orange colour of the rhizome. This colouring comes from a pigment called curcumin, a polyphenol. Turmeric is a member of the ginger family (*Zingiberaceae*), commonly used as a colouring and a flavouring, as well as a dye.

Turmeric is a perennial, normally grown or sown at the end of the rainy season (September) and ready to harvest in the summer (June).

It is not always easy to buy fresh turmeric, although with growing demand we are beginning to see it more in supermarkets (grocery stores). The ground spice is readily available.

I use turmeric for its health benefits, taste and colour. It is delicious as fresh juice, or ground and mixed with warm milk.

Recipes: pages 75, 89, 110, 120, 152

GINGER *Zingiber officinale*
NATIVE TO: *China and South Asia.*

Grown in the tropics, it likes hot weather, and is harvested throughout the year, though it takes around five months for the root to be ready. Ginger is very easy to grow in the right climate, but you can also grow it in the northern hemisphere. I feel that ginger needs recategorizing, as gingers from various countries tastes so different.

When buying or working with ginger, note where it has come from; the source can make a huge difference. An organic ginger from Indonesia will be extremely different from ginger grown in Southern India. Bigger is not better. I find the smaller, denser roots usually pack more punch, intensity and flavour. Organically grown ginger from Kerala in Southern India, known as 'cochin ginger', is juicy and vibrant; Jamaican ginger is also wonderful: intense and fragrant. I avoid mass-produced commercially grown ginger.

Recipes: pages 75, 115, 124, 129, 152, 171

BLACK PEPPER *Piper nigrum*
OTHER NAMES: *the king of spices*
NATIVE TO: *Southern India, also grown across Asia and parts of Africa.*

For a king, it is somewhat taken for granted. I often ask people to take a freshly harvested black peppercorn, slowly chew and taste its qualities. It's a beautiful spice.

It is a tropical plant that flourishes in humidity and loves rain. After flowering, it takes nine months for the fruit (unprocessed green peppercorns) to mature. Clusters of peppercorns are harvested, dried or sometimes immersed in boiling water for a short period (here they turn black) before drying in the sun. Black pepper is packed with therapeutic plant secondary metabolites such as piperine, an alkaloid that gives it zing and bite.

It stimulates digestive secretions, hence why we serve it with food. In Ayurvedic medicine, you take medicinal herbs with black pepper to help absorb the therapeutic constituents.

Recipes: pages 75, 89, 98, 120, 123, 148, 152

Clockwise, from top left: cardamom; black pepper; turmeric

CARDAMOM *Elettaria cardamomum*
OTHER NAMES: *queen of spices, ela in Sanskrit*
NATIVE TO: *Southern and South-east Asia; it grows well in Southern India, Sri Lanka, Malaysia and Indonesia.*

The Malabar Coast in Kerala is the spiritual home of cardamom. A member of the ginger family (*Zingiberaceae*), the plant produces beautiful white and purple flowers and a green fruit. It is this fruit capsule that contains the aromatic black seeds. Cardamom does not fruit until its second or third year. It is planted during the rainy seasons (June and July) and harvested from October to early the following year.

Cardamom is mentioned in the ancient Ayurvedic texts. Arab traders had a penchant for it and merchants took cardamom around the world; it still forms an integral part of a traditional Arabic coffee.

I use cardamom for its aromatic, digestive calming properties, which are due to the high essential oil content (a seed makes a brilliant breath freshener and settles digestion), and for its flavour and aroma.

Recipes: pages 84, 95, 100, 123, 129, 148, 156

CAYENNE *Capsicum minimum*
OTHER NAMES: *Guinea pepper*
NATIVE TO: *Central and South America, now grown and cultivated in Asia, Southern Europe and Australia.*

A member of the *Solanaceae* family, along with potatoes and tobacco, a perennial shrub that bears fruits in the form of red chilli peppers (chiles), which are normally harvested and dried, then powdered.

Cayenne is traditionally used in Asian and South American cuisine. It was used by Native Americans for thousands of years for pain relief and peripheral circulation and is still used for this now. It helps to bring blood to the surface when applied externally or internally. Cayenne loves the heat and brings the heat to a plant potion. I use it for its warming peripheral circulatory stimulating properties and to get things going, particularly in the mornings.

Recipes: pages 69, 95, 118, 123, 126, 136

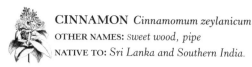

CINNAMON *Cinnamomum zeylanicum*
OTHER NAMES: *sweet wood, pipe*
NATIVE TO: *Sri Lanka and Southern India.*

The sweet-smelling bark is harvested and dried (it curls up into a quill shape) and widely used for culinary purposes, but cinnamon also has a long history of medicinal and cultural use, particularly in Chinese and Ayurvedic practice. Almost every part of the tree, buds, leaves, fruits, flowers and roots can be used.

I love cinnamon, it is a brilliant and dynamic tree, but be careful where you source it as, due to demand, companies are stripping immature trees.

The trees need to mature and should be left to recover from a harvest. The more mature the tree, the better depth of flavour and more volatile oils you will have; the more thoughtful producers will allow their trees to mature fully and also give them time to recover from every harvest.

We must think about where these spices come from, we have taken them for granted for too long; we just expect them to be there on the supermarket (grocery store) shelf whenever we want them. We need to show more respect.

Recipes: pages 84, 95, 115, 123, 148, 166, 171

MASTIC *Pistacia lentiscus*
OTHER NAMES: *gum mastic*
NATIVE TO: *Southern Europe, the Mediterranean, North Africa and West Asia.*

Mastic produces a resin that exudes from the tree and is collected from the bark during the summer months. The resin is sun-dried to form 'mastic tears', which are translucent, slightly yellow drops of resin that can be chewed like a gum.

Mastic gum has an aromatic bitter-like quality that leads into a gentle pine and cedar-like taste. In many cultures in North Africa they traditionally chew the resin; it now forms a part of many formulas for manufactured gum and ice cream all over North Africa and the Middle East. It is thought that the name originally came from the Greek verb *mastichien*, meaning to chew.

Used in traditional Egyptian and Greek medicine

for digestive issues, it has also formed a key part of traditional ceremonial Egyptian incense and perfume blends.

Recipes: pages 115, 148, 166

FRANKINCENSE *Boswellia spp*
NAMES: *olibanum, luban, Boswellia*
NATIVE TO: *Oman, Sudan, Yemen, Somalia, Ethiopia and across the Arabian Peninsula.*

A highly aromatic resin collected from Boswellia trees. There are three main varieties, although *B. sacra* is highly sought-after for its high content of therapeutic oils. The resin is collected from the bark of the trees, dried and graded.

Frankincense has a long and powerful history, used in religious ceremonies. An integral part of ancient Egyptian perfume and incense blends and Greek medicinal preparations, it is now used internally for joint and muscle inflammation, digestive issues and is still highly prized as a fragrance.

Recipes: pages 148, 158, 166

POMEGRANATE *Punica granatum*
OTHER NAMES: *fruit of paradise*
NATIVE TO: *Iran, Northern India and Central Asia, but now dispersed around the Middle East, the Mediterranean and the Americas.*

The pomegranate now has more than 500 cultivars. The trees produce beautiful red flowers and large leather-like berries which contain delicious polyphenol-rich seeds surrounded by red juice-filled sacks called arils. I've ruined many a shirt puncturing those arils.

It has long been seen as a symbol of love. The name Punica is a feminized name for an ancient city in Tunisia where, apparently, the best pomegranates would grow. The fruits ripen six or seven months after the trees have flowered, and this is when the fruits should be harvested.

The leathery fruit capsule was traditionally used by the Greeks and Egyptians for its tannin content, to treat inflammation and digestive issues. The juice is packed full of an array of antioxidant-rich plant chemicals, used to treat heart conditions and peripheral circulation. It's delicious to boot, which makes it a very useful plant from which to create some fantastic plant potions.

Recipes: pages 100, 124

SANDALWOOD *Santalum album*
OTHER NAMES: *white saunders, sanders wood*
NATIVE TO: *India and parts of South-east Asia.*

The heartwood of the tree is prized for its aromatic oils, which produce an amazing perfume. The wood is distilled to create the oil and I think it one of the finest scents in the world. We need to be careful and respect the sandalwood, as they are now endangered.

Steps have been taken to preserve it and much of the sandalwood on the market now is coming from sustainable forests in Australia (from a slightly different species, *Santalum spicatum*). There is a concerted effort to create a more sustainable environment where sandalwood trees can flourish in India and Asia.

Be careful if purchasing sandalwood chips, wood or oil, as much of the 'sandal' on the market is not actually sandalwood. Once you have smelt real *Santalum album* you can never mistake it: a pale heartwood with a breathtakingly beautiful aroma. I use it in some special plant potions, but only in very small quantities.

Recipe: page 114

PROCESSING

We depend on plants for the air we breathe, for 'primary metabolites' – carbohydrates, proteins and fats – but also for a raft of plant chemicals (phytochemicals), or 'secondary metabolites'.

These consist of a huge range of phytochemicals with a wide range of functions: protecting the plant from herbivores, fighting against infection, and attracting pollinating insects. Secondary metabolites include tannins, aromatic oils, alkaloids, resins and steroids that carry a great many potential health benefits for humans, and also a huge palette of flavours, textures and aromas to create delicious potions.

Over the years, our ancestors developed ways to prepare plants to capture both their primary and secondary metabolites. In this section, I am going to explain some of my favourite and essential plant processes, showing you simple techniques so you can enjoy creating potions at home.

Although I enjoy harvesting plants, it is in the alchemical processing of them where I truly come to life. It gives us the opportunity to create a multitude of beautiful, dynamic plant potions.

We work with plants to bring out their greatest qualities, extracting or preserving their flavours, aromas and textures, or capturing the most vibrant aromatic scents from a flower.

We have developed a dynamic relationship with the nature that surrounds us; whether it's collecting and drying plants, creating tinctures from them, or leaving them out to ferment.

Sterilizing equipment

Make sure all bottle and jars are sterilized before use. The best way to do this is to put them through a dishwasher on a high setting. If you have no dishwasher, place bottles or jars in gently boiling water for 5 minutes. Make sure they are completely dry before use.

...and for the time poor

Understandably, we have not all got the time or resources to process our own plants. Luckily, these days we have some great retailers wherever we may be in the world. I give a list of recommended suppliers on page 190.

HARVESTING AND DRYING

I urge you to go outside, build relationships with the nature that surrounds you, whether you are in an urban environment, a desert, or high on a mountain. Walk through your neighbourhood, get to know the trees, plants and weeds.

If you are picking herbs, always stick to those that you know and can easily identify. If you find a plant you do not know, take a picture of it, make notes, or cut a small sample and use these to identify it before even attempting to harvest.

When collecting plants, I tend to go just with an empty bag and notebook, but a sturdy pair of scissors and a pocket knife can come in handy. Sometimes I visualize what I am going to harvest; other times I go with an open heart and mind and see which plants draw my attention.

If you are foraging and harvesting, here's some essential advice:

• Always consider the environment and the plants. Ask yourself: what impact am I going to have? Be conscious of the need to limit damage to the plant and surrounding area; after we leave, a harvesting site needs to look like we haven't been there.

• Although to some it may seem crazy, my ancestors and teachers always told me to take a little time to be with the plant I am harvesting and, without fail, I ask a plant's permission before taking anything. Gather from the healthier plants you find and at the right time of the year (see page 42), making sure always to leave enough for it to continue to grow and flourish. If you find only one small plant of a particular species, leave it alone; go back next year and you may find a new flourishing community that you can then share.

• Any plant collecting, particularly in urban environments, needs to be as far from pollution as possible, so avoid roadsides. Also, check to see whether the area is sprayed with pesticides or weed killers; this is more common in rural areas. If either have been used, stay away, as the sprays will be resistant to water washing. Make sure you collect plants away from any animal's fouling; if unsure, wash with clean water and dry thoroughly with towels. Once harvested, check the plants for insects. Make sure you are not trespassing, and apply for any required permission to harvest.

• Always correctly identify plants before harvesting and utilising; if you're unsure, take a picture and identify it once you are home. If you're in any doubt about the identity of a plant, avoid using it, as some plants are poisonous.

For centuries, we have developed an understanding about which parts of each plant we should harvest and when. For example, I like to collect and process hawthorn berries throughout their season (late summer into autumn / fall), as I believe that you are then able to capture the diverse mixture of constituents and flavours across the plant's development. In summer the hawthorn berries will be green in their infancy, before turning bright red. These young bright red berries not only have a tart vibrancy of flavour, but also yield a very different set of secondary metabolites compared to the sweeter, softer, fully ripened crimson hawthorn berries of autumn (fall).

I do the same with many plants, for example picking the younger, fresher leaves of yarrow as they sprout in spring and the more developed leaves unfurling late into summer and early autumn (fall). As with the hawthorn berries, the differently aged leaves will contain a different mixture of secondary metabolites and flavours to capture during the course of the plant's development. I can then process and use them separately, or combine them to create an ultimate yarrow preparation.

If you are not collecting a plant with flowers, then in most cases it should be harvested before it blooms; always remember to be courteous and only take what you need.

Different parts of the plant should be harvested and processed at different times of the year, for example leaves such as nettle – although good throughout the growing year – are best harvested in spring when the plant's energy is rising to its extremities and the secondary metabolites are at their most potent. But the roots of plants such as dandelion are best harvested in autumn (fall), when the plant's energy returns to the ground in preparation for winter.

The ultimate goal of drying herbs is to capture and maintain the vitality and potency of their flavours, aromatics and constituents for as long as possible. Dried plants should still resemble the fresh version. Drying herbs is an art form that requires care and attention, so you need to use the correct methods to remove their water, while maintaining as much of their potency as possible.

So, it's important that we start the drying process as soon as we can, immediately after harvesting, and always handle the herbs with care and the utmost respect, like a true beloved friend.

Methods of Drying

One of the best, most basic and inexpensive forms of drying, which allows us to dry plants almost anywhere, is the bundling and hanging technique. Bundle the herbs in small manageable bundles, tie them at the base away from the head/flowers with string, fishing line or cotton, and hang them in a dry, dark, well-ventilated place, ideally with circulating warm air. It's important that the space is not too hot, so you don't end up roasting the herbs; also make sure you give the bundles enough room to dehydrate, spacing them really well apart.

So, do check on your drying herbs; it may be a particularly warm or cold period, so drying times will vary, and do make sure the plant material is completely dry before storing, otherwise it will be prone to bacterial degradation and fermentation.

Larger whole roots of plants can also be bundled. As roots are dense, they need longer drying times. I tend to hang whole roots to reduce the water content for a week or so; once they have reduced in

size, I break them down into smaller pieces and dry them for 24 hours in an electric dehydrator, until completely dry.

Drying Racks and Dehydrators

If you have the space, creating a drying rack is a simple but excellent way of drying herbs. These are simple structures, wooden shelves stacked up with adequate distance between each, made from wood with muslin (cheesecloth) stapled to the frames to create a canvas. Carefully place the plants across the canvas, giving enough space for each to dry. For flower heads, such as calendula, this is perfect, just space them out and turn every few days. It is also a great method for drying fruits, berries, barks and smaller pieces of root, as you are not able to bundle and hang them.

A more modern approach is to use electric dehydrators; these are great if you do not have the space that a drying rack requires. They are particularly useful for drying flower heads, berries, fruits, smaller roots, separate leaves and smaller quantities of plants.

Purchasing

Try to imagine the amount of time, love, effort and cost it takes to grow, nurture, harvest, process, pack and deliver just 1kg (2lb 4oz) of dried plant material. Sadly, because many of the plants and dried herbs we encounter in the modern world are trapped inside packaging, tea bags or boxes, we have lost our vital connection with them, and perhaps some of our respect, too.

If you are buying dried herbs, always enquire about their harvest. When were they harvested? And where? You want to have access to the plants as soon as you can after harvest, as dried plants immediately start to lose their vitality. Across the world, sadly, the marketplace is littered with mass-produced, chemically grown, dried herbs. However, wherever you are, there will always be a source of good-quality freshly harvested and processed herbs available; you may have to pay slightly more, but it's worth it.

Drying herbs (from left to right): melissa (lemon balm); yarrow; two bunches of German chamomile

Drying herbs using a dehydrator (left to right): calendula, nettle, ginkgo, elderflower; drying herbs using a drying rack (top to bottom): calendula, Roman chamomile, rose

Also, it's important to look at how herbs are being stored. They should not be in clear glass or plastic containers on display in the light, even if it does look good… for a short time, anyway. These herbs will soon grow brown, old and dusty, losing their vitality.

If you have taken the trouble to harvest and dry herbs, you should seal them in airtight containers away from any natural light. Although it is lovely to be able to see your dried herbs – and not the end of the world if you do use clear glass containers – ideally you want to store them in non-porous, airtight ziplock bags or boxes.

If you do choose clear glass, try to store the containers away from light. However you store them, I recommend using dried herbs within one year of purchase or harvest.

Powdered herbs

Once you have dried your herbs, or if you have bought whole dried herbs, you may wish to powder them. This is particularly useful for any extraction process, because it allows the maximum amount of plant material to be in contact with as much of the solvent as possible.

I'm not keen on powdering herbs to store for the long term, but instead just as and when you need them, as it's best for the vitality of the plant and its constituents to keep it as whole as possible for as long as possible.

The best ways to powder herbs are either in a large old-fashioned mortar and pestle, or in hand-held or electric coffee grinders, or in a Vitamix or similar blender; the last is particularly useful if you have tough dried roots to powder. Of course, you can also purchase many herbs in powdered form. If you have excess powder, or if you have bought powder, make sure it is kept in an airtight container in a dry, cool place.

WATER

The ultimate solvent and the most important life force of nature, essential to all life … yet it is becoming increasingly challenging to find good sources of water, particularly in our urban environments. Crazily, it has been taken for granted, or treated as a commodity. Water has been used from our very beginnings for all alchemical preparations, and all recipes in this book require water in some form.

It is important to work with a good source of pure water. If you have access to pure spring, well or river water, then great! (A little research may surprise you here, there may be a pure source of water closer to you than you think.) If not, then I'd recommend a simple water filter, even a piece of activated charcoal. (There are also other techniques for re-energizing water, see pages 84 and 168.) If you only have access to drinking water from the mains, that's fine, but you may wish to boil the water before using it for any preparations.

I use distilled water in many recipes, as the distillation process gives me a blank canvas with which to work. It's neutral, as all impurities, character and mineral content have been stripped out during the distillation process. It also means that my plant preparations have an extended shelf life, as there is little or no bacteria present in the water that might bring on early spoilage. Distilled water is easy and inexpensive to buy.

Brewing Hot & Cold

Brewing, or infusing plants in hot or cold water for a period of time, is a basic but most beautiful art. It is still very hard to beat the taste. Various flavours and constituents of herbs will leach out and infuse the water at different temperatures and over varying infusion times.

For example, a cold infusion of Roman chamomile will result in very little flavour, but in very hot water you can actually see its constituents and flavours: it will turn yellow, then blue after a longer infusion time, and taste bitter and aromatic. On the flip side, hot water infusions of lavender can become overpowering, so I prefer a gentle cold or room temperature water infusion here.

HOT BREWING

'Blooming' is a term common in coffee brewing, and relates to releasing the carbon dioxide from the freshly roasted coffee beans by dampening them, allowing the beans to take in hot water and, conversely, to give up their flavours and aromas to the water. In a similar way, by soaking a little plant material in hot water, its tissues swell and allow its constituents, flavours and aromas to disperse into water more readily. This is useful with dried berries, powdered herbs and shredded hard roots.

To brew a herbal infusion using dried herbs, place 3 heaped teaspoons of the herbs into a teapot, gently pour a small amount (about 50ml / 2fl oz / scant ¼ cup) of freshly boiled water over all of the herbs to cover, then let them soak and expand for 30 seconds. Now gently pour another 200ml (7fl oz / scant 1 cup) of water into the pot and cover with a lid, so as not to lose any aromatics to evaporation. Infuse for a good 5 minutes, but use your intuition; experiment, you may prefer the taste of some plants after a shorter infusion time, and others after a longer wait, particularly if you are steeping harder roots, barks and seeds.

As a general rule, tough plant material: barks such as cinnamon; roots such as dandelion; or dense flower heads such as Roman chamomile;

Preparing an infusion of calendula and rose

are better infused for slightly longer, so water can penetrate and draw out the flavours. Greener, lighter fragrant leaves such as peppermint or sage, or lighter flowers or petals such as rose or lavender, only require a shorter infusion time. It's important to note that, with almost all herbs, you can infuse them more than once; it is wasteful to discard herbs that have only been infused once. Roman chamomile will often improve on the third or even fourth infusion, as its flavours and constituents slowly leach out from deep within the herb.

I like to steep hardier parts of plants, such as cinnamon, in hot water with the lid on and leave them overnight, to be drunk either cold or warmed up the following day. This produces a really powerful and delicious brew packed full of vibrant flavours, plus a diverse range of secondary metabolites, due to the longer infusion time.

As a general rule, I suggest infusing herbs, fresh or dried, with freshly boiled water, for at least 5–8 minutes in a teapot with the lid on.

A note on brewing fresh herbs: there is nothing quite so delicious as a pot of freshly harvested herbs or spices. But fresh herbs contain lots of water, so if you want to change a recipe for a dried herb infusion to the fresh version, I recommend doubling the quantity of fresh herbs in the teapot and using much cooler water.

In terms of temperature, I use mostly just-off-the-boil water at 96–98°C (205–208°F) for dried herbs and a slightly cooler 85–90°C (185–194°F) for fresh. However, it is dependent on the plant; for example, for an aromatic extraction of lavender I use cooler water, as it can get overpowering.

COLD DRIPPING

This method yields really beautiful results. As I write, I am enjoying a glass of slowly dripped sage. It's utterly delicious.

You will need: *50g (1¾oz) coarsely ground herbs; 500ml (18fl oz / generous 2 cups) spring water*

Pack the bottom section of a cold dripper with the herbs, then soak with 50ml (2fl oz / scant ¼ cup) of the water to expand and open up the herbs for 30 seconds or so. Place a moistened paper filter on top, then slowly drip spring water through at the rate of 1 drop every 3 seconds; this should take around 4 hours to drip through. Drink immediately or bottle and seal. It keeps, chilled, for up to 3 days.

COLD / ROOM TEMPERATURE BREWING

I find there is nothing like a cold infusion of mint and sage with a touch of wormwood to cool you down. Brewing herbs is not rocket science: use your intuition; look at the herb you are working with; use your senses of taste, smell, sight and touch. What I offer you here are just guidelines to inspire you.

If you want a lighter, more refreshing infusion, brewing at cold or room temperatures works very well with aromatic plants such as mint, thyme, lemon balm and sage, as their aromatic secondary metabolites infuse with cold water beautifully, without the pungent bitter notes that hot water infusions can sometimes produce.

You will need: 4–5 heaped teaspoons of dried herbs, or 6–7 heaped teaspoons of fresh herbs, 750ml–1 litre (1¼–1¾ pints / 3¼–4 cups) spring water, cold or at room temperature

Place the herbs in a glass jug (pitcher), gently pour over a little of the cold or room temperature water to soak or bloom the herbs, leave for 30 seconds, then carefully add the rest of the water. Stir and leave for at least a couple of hours, stirring occasionally. If you are in a hot climate you can leave the jug in the refrigerator, or you might want to leave it outside to capture the vibrancy of the Sun, before chilling later to enjoy with friends. Depending on the herbs, you may wish to leave it for longer. I tend to prefer stronger flavours, so I'll leave an infusion overnight, or prepare it first thing in the morning to enjoy in the afternoon. Once the water has been infused, you can seal it in a beautiful glass bottle or decanter and keep it in the refrigerator for a few days.

For a simple sparkling infusion, gently pour ground herbs into a bottle of sparkling water (carefully pour off a little of the water first, if necessary), seal the lid and leave for several hours, then strain through a tea strainer to serve.

Juicing Herbs

Perhaps the ultimate way to enjoy the plants around us is to ingest them immediately after harvesting or purchasing, capturing their maximum vitality and energy. Juicing is particularly great in spring, as there are many nutritious revitalizing, cleansing herbs about, such as nettle, cleavers and plantain, bursting with mineral-rich primary and secondary metabolites. The key to juicing is to pick the best-quality fresh herbs, fruits and produce, then juice or press them as quickly as possible.

I use a masticating juicer. When travelling or in the field, I use a hand-held crank-operated juicer that does the same job. You don't need to spend lots of money on juicers, you can even use a simple old-fashioned apple press for your fruits and vegetables. This is a simple press used for centuries by many cultures to press grapes, other fruits, or other plants. It exerts pressure on plant material through a screw press, separating the liquid from the solids, extracting the juice and oils from a plant without the damage and degradation that can be caused by the heat of the speeding blades used in many commercial juicers.

Importantly, when it comes to fresh herbs – and, in particular, citrus fruits – not only do we want as much of the juice as possible, but also the vibrant therapeutic, aromatic oils found in the leaves, flowers and skins. To extract these oils from fresh herbs and citrus, I find that masticating juicers are the best choice.

Juicing rules:
- *Use a masticating, screw press or hydraulic press juicer.*
- *Use great produce, or freshly grown or harvested herbs.*
- *Juice the herbs or produce as soon as you can after picking or buying them.*
- *Pass a little fresh water through the juicer after juicing, to collect the remaining juices and oils.*
- *Freeze juice in ice trays to use in autumn (fall) and winter, when plants cannot be found fresh.*

It's important to use leftover pulp from a juicer. It makes great plant fertilizer. Be creative: you could use it to create infused herbal vinegar, or even try to ferment it (see right).

Fermentation

One of the most basic and fundamental processes on the planet; the oldest form of biotechnology, if you like. Fermentation requires little-to-no specialist equipment and this dynamic microbial and enzymatic transformation will occur naturally, or can be controlled using starter cultures.

Without getting too deep into the biochemistry, during fermentation, the carbohydrate in fruits and herbs are transformed by yeasts and bacteria into dynamic mixtures of yeasts, bacterias, organic acids and/or alcohol. The process does not always yield alcohol; the recipes featured in this book may contain small traces of alcohol but are not intended to create alcohol. Cheese- and bread-making both require fermentation but produce negligible amounts of alcohol, as do our own red blood cells.

The fermentation of herbs, fruits and honey were among the world's first alchemical preparations: plants and fruits were harvested and left out for wild bacterias and yeasts in the air to convert their carbohydrates into a complex living cocktail of organic acids, yeasts and bacterias. This enabled people to preserve foods, fruits and drinks, with the added health benefits of enhancing their nutrient content and its absorbability.

Fermented foods contain health-giving probiotic properties. Probiotics are live bacterias and yeasts that enhance the positive microbial balance of the gastrointestinal tract. This is associated with a raft of positive health benefits, such as an increase in nutrient assimilation, reduced inflammation and enhanced immune function.

Some of the earliest fermented foods – kimchi, sauerkraut, Chinese tea (kombucha) and natto (soy bean) – transformed the diet of our ancestors through their flavours, textures and aromas.

The art of fermentation has reached new heights with a global explosion in popularity of ancient 'living' drinks, such as kombucha, jun or kefir. Here is a simple lacto-fermented herb recipe: please experiment, have fun with the wild yeasts and bacterias that fill the air around you, and the starter cultures easily found wherever you are in the world.

LACTO-FERMENTED HERBS

This converts sugars into lactic acid, for a delicious probiotic potion. I'm using this mixture of herbs as I like their taste with carrot juice, but please do experiment.

You will need: 8 (or enough to make 500ml /18fl oz / generous 2 cups of juice) carrots, with tops if you can; ½ beetroot; 1 good handful of fresh mixed herbs (dill / tarragon / lemon balm / thyme); 1 heaped teaspoon sea salt

Juice the carrots, beetroot and herbs, strain and pour into a sterilized container. Stir in the salt and seal. Store at room temperature, away from light, for 1 month. Open, decant into a small glass and sip before a meal. This helps stimulate digestion. Once opened, this is best enjoyed within 1 week; though longer fermentations yield interesting flavours.

Tincture & Glycerides

NON-ALCOHOLIC TINCTURES

By tincturing, we are trying to extract the totality of flavours and constituents from a plant into a concentrated liquid, to use in small doses. We can prepare tinctures using fresh and dried herbs, flowers and spices and an extracting liquid of water, glycerine or vinegar.

Please do experiment with these preparations, as you might like a certain type of fresh plant, or a mixture of dried herbs together in different ratios. I will show you a couple of simple recipes and techniques, just to plant a seed, so you can play around with different plants, dried and fresh; with ratios of liquid; varying techniques; or maceration, percolating and decocting times.

Vegetable glycerine is a viscous, colourless, odourless liquid, a component of triglyceride (fat). It is soluble in water and extracted from plants. Although it tastes sweet, it contains no sugar. It is an excellent solvent, a good preservative and you can have lots of fun with it in preparing potions. Source vegetable glycerine, not synthetic glycerine.

BASIC GLYCERITE TINCTURE 1:5

This is a simple, effective way to create a water-soluble concentrated herbal extract.

You will need: 200g (7oz) dried herbs, coarsely powdered; 200ml (7fl oz / scant 1 cup) distilled water; 800ml (1⅓ pints / 3½ cups) vegetable glycerine

Place the ingredients in a blender, blend for 30 seconds, then decant into an airtight sealable jar, seal, shake well and store for at least 14 days (preferably longer), shaking occasionally.

Strain through muslin (cheesecloth) or a super bag, pressing the herb to make sure as much liquid as possible is extracted, then bottle, seal and label. It will keep for at least 6 months.

Water bath: For a little extra extraction and intensity of flavour, you can apply some heat to the mixture, being careful not to cook the preparation. Place the sealed jar into a pot of hot water at 50–60°C (122–140°F) for 1 hour or so twice a week before straining. If you are fortunate enough to have access to a sous-vide machine, you can seal the liquid in a bag and leave at 50°C (122°F) for 3–4 hours, leave in the bag for a further week, then blend the contents, before straining and bottling.

DECOCTION

A preparation that requires heating fresh or dried herbs with water to reduce or boil down. This is useful for the roots and barks of plants whose flavours and constituents are particularly stubborn to extract from the tough plant material. By using heat, you can break down its structure.

Traditional decoctions are boiled aggressively; I favour a slightly gentler approach in my more modern preparations, so as not to risk denaturing or spoiling the extracted flavours of the decoctions with excessive heat.

DECOCTED WATER & GLYCERINE TINCTURE 1:6

Particularly useful for barks; dried roots such as dandelion, ginger and turmeric; or seeds.

You will need: 140g (5oz) dried herbs, coarsely powdered; 400ml (14fl oz / 1¾ cups) distilled water; 400ml (14fl oz / 1¾ cups) vegetable glycerine

Place the herbs and water in a saucepan. If you have time, let them infuse for a couple of hours. Stir, cover, then bring to a rolling gentle boil for 3–4 minutes. Turn off the heat and leave to cool with the lid on. Put it in a blender with the glycerine, blend for 30 seconds, then pour into an airtight sealable container and leave for at least 14 days (I prefer a full moon cycle), shaking occasionally. Strain through muslin (cheesecloth) or a super bag and bottle.

DRIP-PERCOLATED WATER & GLYCERINE TINCTURE 1:4

A highly concentrated dual-extracted tincture, combining gentle percolation with a more intense glycerine extraction.

You will need: 100g (3½oz) dried herbs, coarsely powdered; 200ml (7fl oz / scant 1 cup) distilled water; 200ml (7fl oz / scant 1 cup) vegetable glycerine

Pack half the herbs into the bottom of a cold-dripper, soak or bloom (see page 47) with about 50ml (2fl oz / scant ¼ cup) of the water, then place a moistened filter paper on top. Pour the remaining water into the top and set to drip at 1 drop every 3 seconds.

Pour the liquid, glycerine, remaining herbs and the percolated herbs into a blender. Blend for 30 seconds, then store, shake and strain as above, pressing hard on the herbs.

Bitters

Commonplace in any bar worth its salt over the last century, and one of the most familiar herbal remedies to infiltrate the mainstream drinks industry. Bitters recipes are essentially processed in much the same way as tinctures (see page 53), except they tend to be polypharmic, which means that they contain a complex mixture of herbs and spices, rather than just a couple.

As we know, in processing plants we are trying to extract the flavoursome plant secondary metabolites. These have been stripped away from the plants in our diets through mass breeding and chemically enhanced farming methods. The nature that surrounds us, particularly wild herbs and spices, are a fantastic source of secondary metabolites and – almost without fail – they are bitter in taste.

Take a leaf of wild-grown rocket (arugula) and chew it: it's bitter. Take a leaf of fresh wild dandelion: it's really bitter. Take a tiny leaf of fresh wormwood: it's really, really bitter… You get my point. When creating bitters, we want to work with the more bitter-flavoured plants such as dandelion, gentian, citrus peel, hops, wormwood and Roman chamomile. We balance those bitter flavours with slightly more aromatic plants such as cinnamon, cardamom, lavender and rose… while still retaining the predominantly bitter characteristic of the overall preparation.

Bitters are excellent preparations to take before and after eating, to stimulate the appetite or help to digest a meal. There are a wide range of beneficial actions associated with bitter plant secondary metabolites, such as the metabolism of hormones, the stimulation of neurological tissue in the gut (digestive tract), interactions with immune response, central and peripheral nervous systems, as well as direct antibacterial, malarial and parasitic actions… the list goes on. I find the topic fascinating and could talk forever on it; I won't here, so a list of recommended titles can be found on page 190.

King of Bitters (see page 152)

BASIC BITTERS RECIPE

For the bitter herb blend
You will need: 80g (3oz) dandelion root; 10g (¼oz) lavender flowers; 10g (¼oz) coriander seeds; 50g (1¾oz) fennel seeds; 50g (1¾oz) chamomile flowers

For the bitters
You will need: 1 quantity Bitter Herb Blend; 1 unwaxed lemon, organic if possible, quartered; 200ml (7fl oz / scant 1 cup) distilled water; 800ml (1⅓ pints / 3½ cups) vegetable glycerine

In a coffee grinder, blender, or mortar and pestle, grind everything for the bitter herb blend into a coarse powder.

Place all the ingredients for the bitters into an airtight sealable jar, squeezing the oils from the lemon by pressing the skin between your thumb and index finger, then seal, gently shake and label.

Store for at least 1 month (preferably longer), gently shaking occasionally. Strain through muslin (cheesecloth) or a super bag, pressing the herb blend to make sure as much of the liquid is strained off as possible.

Bottle in a dropper bottle, seal and label. This will keep for at least 6 months. For a more rapid infusion, place in a water bath, as with Glycerite Tincture (see page 53).

Enjoy 10–15 drops with water, either before or after eating.

Sherbets

From the Persian *sharbat* and the Arabic *shariba*, meaning 'to drink', and based on old formulas of fruits, flowers, seeds and plants mixed with sugar, water and occasionally vinegar. These would often have been prepared using hydrosols such as bitter orange flower, violet or rose. As there was no refrigeration in early times, a syrup of fruits and flowers created a preserved concentrate, which could then be lengthened with water. It is possible that the original sherbet was the precursor to what we know as a 'shrub', a mix of fruit, sugar and vinegar, which has regained popularity in bars and restaurants around the world over the last decade.

I don't mind using sugar as long as it's not too much, it's from a good source and is as unrefined as possible. We had a long relationship with this grass, sugar cane, way before it was processed into something it should never have been.

I love the versatile sweet-and-sour flavours of sherbets, and the way they allow for the integration of herbs and spices into beautiful-tasting drinks. The acidity from citrus is fantastic at extracting flavours, as well as preserving the preparations. Here is a simple recipe, but get creative: if you don't have fresh herbs, use dried, and if you don't want to use sugar, you can use coconut nectar or honey.

BASIC HERBAL SHERBET

You will need: 6 unwaxed lemons, organic if possible; 20g (¾oz) mint leaves; 250g (9oz / 1¼ cups) sugar, coconut nectar or raw honey

---

Pare the zests from the lemons, then put the zests in a container with the herbs and sugar. Muddle or press the zest, leaves and sugar together for a minute or so (I use a mortar and pestle, but a bowl and rolling pin would work),

then juice the lemons and stir the juice into the mixture. Seal and leave to infuse overnight, or for at least 6 hours. Stir, strain and bottle. This will keep refrigerated for at least 1 month.

Enjoy a couple of tablespoons with still or sparkling water, or integrate into other plant potions (see pages 98 and 102).

Herb-infused Honeys & Oxymels

Honey has always been used as both food and medicine, and infusing it is an ancient but beautiful way to preserve and extract the flavour and constituents from dried, fresh or powdered herbs. Unrefined natural honey is known as a fantastic natural preservative; the composition of each batch varies depending on the plants the bees used, the environment and how it has been processed, but find a good local source.

Honey is a super-saturated solution of natural sugars (fructose and glucose), macro- and micro-nutrients, and amino acids, with many potential health-giving benefits. Besides that, I find it utterly delicious and a beautiful expression of the nature that surrounds us. Of course, it's important that we are conscious about over-using honey, as bee colonies are struggling worldwide, but as long as you support local beekeepers who in turn support local bee colonies, I believe that can only help strengthen both bees and the local flora.

The great thing about herb-infused honeys is that they are so easy to prepare that I often make them if I have leftover herbs and flowers.

SAGE-INFUSED HONEY

This is a simple sage-infused honey; you can use this recipe as a blueprint.

You will need: 100g (3½oz) fresh, dried or powdered sage (if it's fresh, cut it into pieces); 300g (10½oz / 1 cup) raw honey

Put the sage into a 500ml (18fl oz / 2 generous cups) glass jar, cover with honey, stir and seal.

Place the sealed jar in a water bath, or in a pot, with warm water at 50°C (122°F), just to help the infusion get underway. Be careful not to heat it too much, as you don't want to denature and lose the nutrient content of the honey. Warm through for 15–20 minutes, gently shaking, then remove from the water and store in a dark cupboard or airing cupboard. Leave for at least 14 days, but the longer the better. I've kept plants in honey for years, it is always delightful. If you are concerned about the plant material floating around, warm up the honey and strain it through muslin (cheesecloth) or a super bag once you have finished infusing.

OXYMELS

From the Latin *oxymeli*, 'acid and honey', I'm
pleased to say I've noticed a bit of a resurgence
of this ancient technique. The basic premise is
similar to an infused honey, but with the added
extracting power and flavour of vinegar to create a
wonderful sweet-and-sour infusion. My preferred
vinegar is a living apple cider vinegar, because of its
diverse array of organic acids; I also love the taste in
combination with honey.

*You will need: 100g (3½oz) fresh or dried herbs;
300g (10½oz / 1 cup) raw honey; 150ml (5fl oz / ⅔
cup) cider vinegar*

In a 500ml (18fl oz) jar, put your choice of herbs,
cover with honey and vinegar, stir and seal. Process
in a 50°C (122°F) water bath and store as for
the infused honey (see left). Keep for at least 14
days, longer if possible, and, again, strain if you
prefer. You may wish to adjust the ratio of honey to
vinegar, depending on which you are using.

Hydrosols

I am very much inspired by the ancient art of distillation and the Middle Eastern distillers of the ninth and tenth centuries. I work with hydrosols (aromatic waters) almost every day, in fact they have changed my life. I was given a fresh water distillation of *Rosa damascena*; it was so profound that our daughter was named Damascena.

Hydrosols (*hydro* meaning water and *sol* meaning solution) are often by-products from essential oil production, but I distil hydrosols as the primary product, by prolonged distilling at much lower temperatures than for essential oils.

Hydrosols are non-alcoholic water extractions of pure plant material, a very simple and fundamental process. The plant material is added to water in a still, which is heated from below. After a time, aromatic vapours rise up, condense, cool and turn back into aromatized water: magic! It is an art, and should you wish to read further, take a look at my list of references (see page 190).

The first alembic stills – two vessels connected by a tube – were traditionally made from copper or clay, but nowadays (sadly) you are more likely to find them made from stainless steel or glass. I say 'sadly' as I'm a firm believer in the use of copper, and love the interaction or 'conversation' between copper, water, nature and the plants. Copper is alive, it lives, breathes and converses with its environment (see page 84).

A popular modern extraction method used by scientists, which has gained popularity with chefs and bartenders, is the 'rotovap', or rotary evaporator system, that works using carefully controlled temperature and pressure changes that allow the user to meticulously extract aromatic plant compounds and aromatic waters. I have experimented with these systems with some very interesting and often brilliant results, however, it's an expensive piece of kit and not something everyone can use at home!

To start your distillation journey, collect or purchase the plant material; ideally fresh, but dried can be used if you follow my guidelines on drying or sourcing dried herbs (see page 41). The beauty of distillation is there are no set rules, so do please experiment and get to know the plants you are working with.

As a rough guide, use three times as much water as plant material, so, if you have 2kg (4½lb) of plant material, use 6 litres (10½ pints / 6.3 quarts) of fresh water. However, as you dive into the art of distillation, you will experiment and find that certain plants require more or less water. Add the pure water to the bottom of the still, along with the plant material. This can either be submerged in the water, or placed in the neck of the still, or both. The still is then heated from below – butane gas is great for this as you can control it – and, as the mixture of water and plant material heats up, the volatile and non-volatile constituents and essences from the plants vaporize into the steam and rise to the top of the still.

As the steam rises to the top (called the 'swan's neck', for obvious reasons), it starts to cool, condense, then drip back as a liquid into a condenser unit that is filled with cool water.

After a time, depending on how much water and plant material you are using, and the temperature you are distilling at, out will drop a harmonious blend of plant constituent-enriched aromatic water. It will contain varying qualities and constituents at different times of the distillation, which may run for several hours, again depending on the quantity of water and plant material. Bottle, label and store the aromatic water in a glass bottle in a cool dark place or, even better, in the refrigerator. Hydrosols keep for a year; some keep for longer and even improve with age, but generally they are best enjoyed fresh.

These are very basic guidelines for distilling, I just wanted to 'light the fire', inspire the next alchemist who may be reading this. (Further resources for distilling, purchasing stills and equipment can be found on page 190.)

These beautiful hydrosols are brilliantly dynamic tools for creating the most delicious plant potions.

Clean equipment

I know it's not the most exciting part, but it is imperative that all equipment is spotlessly clean before and after distilling. I was taught how to distil by one of France's leading *eau de vie* distillers. One of the first things he taught me was to be clean, and how much of the work in distilling is cleaning. So be sure to scrub the still clean with hot water before and after each distillation, then cleanse by spraying and wiping, either with a neutral grain alcohol solution of around 70% ABV, or citric acid, before rinsing with distilled water.

CO2 EXTRACTION

One of the more contemporary methods of extracting flavours and oils from plants. I work with it a great deal, as it gives beautifully clean, vibrant extraction of oils and constituents.

CO_2 is condensed under high pressure and controlled temperature, so it changes its density, surface tension and viscosity into what is called a 'supercritical fluid'. This dissolves oils and active compounds from plant material… then just evaporates when pressure is reduced, leaving behind the aromatic extracted oils.

You can buy desktop CO_2 extractors, though at great cost, but good-quality essential oil retailers now sell extracts produced using CO_2 extraction (see page 190). Choose your provider carefully. Also, please note, as with essential oils, these are very concentrated extracts with powerful effects and flavours, so must be handled with respect and care.

THE DRINKS

Here is a collection of some of my favourite plant potions, elixirs and tonics for you to enjoy making at home for your friends and family. These recipes are just guidelines… I do urge you to be creative with them, to use the recipes to inspire you to create your own drinks from our glorious wealth of plants. Above all, have fun.

Cleansing Infusion

Cleansing

Skin Tonic

Cleansing Infusion

A simple amalgamation of some of my favourite cleansing herbs in a delicious herbal tea that can be enjoyed throughout the year. This infusion is particularly delicious in the morning, but can be prepared in a large batch and heated up as and when required.

   If you are collecting the plants yourself, please have a look at my tips on harvesting and drying herbs (see page 41). If you are purchasing dried herbs, consult my list of recommended suppliers (see page 190). Further information on all these plants can be found on pages 16–39.

Makes 1 tea caddy, or enough for about 20 teapots

100g (3½oz) dried calendula flowers
75g (2¾oz) dried nettle leaf
50g (1¾oz) dried cleavers
50g (1¾oz) dried horsetail
50g (1¾oz) dried red clover
25g (1oz) dried fennel seed
50g (1¾oz) dried burdock root

Weigh out all the dried herbs and mix together in a large bowl. Decant into an airtight container and seal. As with all dried herbs, this mixture will keep for 1 year in the sealed container.

Measure out 3–4 tsp of the herb mixture into a teapot, just cover the herbs with freshly boiled water and leave for 30 seconds to allow them to 'bloom' (see page 47), then top up with more just-boiled water and place the lid on the pot. Allow to infuse for at least 5 minutes, then pour through a tea strainer into cups and enjoy.

Skin Tonic

Good morning! This invigorating drink is a step up from that well-known simple morning ritual of lemon and hot water, helping circulation and firing up the digestion with its combination of warming ginger and cayenne with stimulating dandelion and burdock.

Dandelion and burdock have antioxidant, anti-inflammatory and gentle bitter actions, which make this drink an essential part of a cleansing routine. The two are among my favourite skin herbs, due to their diuretic actions (in France, dandelion is known as *pis-en-lit* or 'wet the bed'); they help to regulate blood pressure, cleansing the kidneys, bladder and urinary system. Please note: I have *never* wet the bed after consuming dandelion, nor do I know anyone who has, so do not let this put you off!

MAKES 1 TEAPOT

For the drink
2.5cm (1in) fresh organic
    ginger root
1 unwaxed or organic lemon, finely
    grated zest and juice
pinch of cayenne pepper
dash of raw honey or alternative
    sweetener (optional)
2ml (½ tsp) Dandelion and Burdock
    Decocted Tincture (see below)

**For the Dandelion and Burdock
Decocted Tincture (makes
about 500ml / 18fl oz / generous
2 cups)**
40g (1½oz) dried dandelion root
40g (1½oz) dried burdock root
250ml (9fl oz / generous 1 cup)
    distilled water
300ml (10fl oz / 1¼ cups) vegetable
    glycerine

*Equipment: muslin cloth
    (cheesecloth) or super bag; 50ml
    (2fl oz) glass bottle with pipette*

For the drink: Cut the ginger into small pieces and place in a teapot. Squeeze in the finely grated zest and juice of half the lemon and add the cayenne pepper and honey or sweetener, if required. Pour over 200ml (7fl oz / scant 1 cup) of freshly boiled water. Leave the lid on the teapot and infuse for 4–5 minutes. Strain through a tea strainer into tea cups, then drop the tincture into each cup from a pipette. Take a small piece of zest from the remaining half lemon and squeeze the oils out over the cups with your thumb and index finger.

For the Dandelion and Burdock Decocted Tincture: Put the dried dandelion and burdock roots into a saucepan with the distilled water (if you have time, let the herbs infuse for a couple of hours before heating). Stir, fire up the heat with the lid on, bring to a gentle simmer for 3–4 minutes, then turn off the heat and leave to cool with the lid on (you don't want to lose any of the aromatics through evaporation). Once cool, add it all to a blender with the glycerine, blend for 30 seconds, then pour into an airtight sealable container and leave to macerate in a cupboard for at least 14 days or one full moon cycle (see page 13), gently shaking occasionally. Strain through muslin (cheesecloth) or a super bag, bottle and label.

Spring Clean

When the energy rises in spring, take advantage of the plants shooting up to capture the warmth. Nettle is packed with chlorophyll and folic acid, while cleavers make a fantastic lymph-cleansing tonic, and both grow across Europe and North America. With a fennel-and-lime-infused honey, this is packed with phytochemicals to detoxify, and promote healthy skin, for the perfect spring clean.

SERVES 1

For the drink
2 good handfuls of fresh nettles and
  cleavers, roughly equal parts
5–6 fresh dandelion flowers
100ml (3½fl oz / 7 tbsp)
  Sun-infused Dandelion Spring
  Water (see below)
1 organic green apple (I used a
  Granny Smith)
35g (1¼oz / heaping 2 tbsp)
  Fennel and Lime Honey
  (see below)
fresh fennel tops and yarrow leaves,
  to serve (optional)

Equipment: masticating juicer

**For the Fennel and Lime Honey
(makes about 100g / 3½oz)**
5 unwaxed or organic limes
2 large pinches of fennel seeds
100g (3½oz / 7 tbsp) local light
  raw honey

*Equipment: muslin cloth
  (cheesecloth) or super bag*

**For the Sun-infused Dandelion
Spring Water (makes 500ml /
18fl oz / generous 2 cups)**
5–6 freshly picked dandelion
  flowers

For the drink: Rinse the herbs. Run the herbs and flowers through a masticating juicer, followed by the Sun-infused Dandelion Spring Water. Slice the apple and run it, too, through the juicer. Measure the honey into a glass, adding ice if you like. Pour over the juice and stir. Garnish with freshly picked fennel tops and / or yarrow leaves, if you like.

For the Fennel and Lime Honey: Remove the zest from 4 of the limes, then juice all the limes. Put the fennel seeds in a saucepan, crush them with your fingers or use the back of a spoon in the pan, then add the lime juice, lime zest and 50ml (2fl oz / scant ¼ cup) of spring water and gently bring to a simmer, while stirring. Simmer for 3–4 minutes, then add the honey for 1 further minute. Stir, remove from the heat and allow to cool. Fine-strain through a muslin cloth (cheesecloth) or super bag, then bottle and seal. A splash of this is also fantastic enjoyed with still or sparkling water.

For a more intensely flavoured infused honey, place the infused honey into a sealed jar without straining and leave for 14 days.

For the Sun-infused Dandelion Spring Water: On a bright spring morning, when flashes of brilliant yellow dandelions are winking at you from the pavements (sidewalks), go out and pick a few of the flower heads. This infused water adds a subtle herbaceous sweetness to the drink, to awaken the body and harmonize the urinary system.

Place the flowers in a sealed jug (pitcher) or glass carafe with 500ml (18fl oz / generous 2 cups) of spring water, stir and seal. Place in the sun for at least 2 hours. Sip throughout the day. Top up after use and re-infuse the flowers until they can no longer be enjoyed.

Note: Fresh herbs and fruits yield different quantities of juice, so the above recipe is just a guideline; you may feel, when you make it, that you need more herbs or more fruit. Also be assured that juicing nettles removes their stinging properties, so you will not be injured during this process! You can also use dried nettles and cleavers: make a strong infusion with hot water (see page 47), then cool, strain and use in place of the fresh-juiced herbs.

Sun-infused Dandelion Spring Water

Spring Tonic

Bright, bold and reinvigorating, this is all about plants that help to shift us out of our winter slumber, get things moving, and add a little spice and intensity to our mornings. It features turmeric, the golden root so important in traditional Indian medicine and cuisine; it's fantastic for the organs of digestion, particularly the liver and gall bladder, and for the absorption of fats and fat-soluble vitamins. The secondary metabolites in pepper and ginger (see page 40) also help us to absorb the therapeutic constituents in turmeric. Combined with antioxidant carotenoids and the high vitamin content of the carrot, as well as the added zing of the orange, this will brighten up any day.

SERVES 1

For the drink
1 organic carrot
1 unwaxed or organic orange
2.5cm (1in) fresh organic ginger root
2.5cm (1in) fresh organic turmeric root (if available)
10ml (2 tsp) Turmeric and Honey (see below)

Equipment: masticating juicer

For the Turmeric and Honey
(makes about 600ml / 1 pint / 2½ cups)
100g (3½oz) dried turmeric root, whole or powdered
15g (½oz) dried ginger root, slices or powdered
15g (½oz) black peppercorns
250ml (9fl oz / generous 1 cup) distilled water
400g (14oz / scant 1½ cups) raw honey

Equipment: muslin cloth (cheesecloth) or super bag

For the Turmeric and Honey: Put the turmeric, ginger and peppercorns in a saucepan with the distilled water. Cover and place over a low heat for 3–4 minutes (do not boil), then allow to cool, still with the lid on. Pour it all into a blender, add the honey, blend for 30 seconds, then decant into an airtight sealable jar. Seal, shake well, label and store for at least 14 days (preferably longer), shaking occasionally. Strain through muslin cloth (cheesecloth) or a super bag, pressing the solids to make sure as much of the liquid as possible is extracted, then bottle, seal and label. This will keep for at least 12 months and can be enjoyed with a splash of water, or just added to a simple orange juice.

For the drink: Wash and peel the carrot, then remove the zest from the orange and set aside. Pass the carrot, orange, one-quarter of the orange zest, the ginger and turmeric (if using) through a masticating juicer, followed by 100ml (3½fl oz / 7 tbsp) of spring water. Pour the juice into a glass with the Turmeric and Honey, stir and serve. This can also be bottled to be enjoyed on the go, or at work.

The Green Pharmacy

For the drink
1 handful of fresh plants and herbs
(plantain, cleavers, nettle and
ground ivy, or use a mixture)
75ml (2½fl oz / 5 tbsp) juice from
    organic apples or pears, pineapple
    or green grapes (optional)
10–20 drops of Parsley, Nettle and
    Peppermint Tincture (see below)
edible wild flowers or herbs,
    to serve (optional)
spritz of Peppermint Hydrosol
    (see page 60)

Equipment: masticating juicer

**For the Parsley, Nettle and
Peppermint Tincture (makes
about 600ml / 1 pint / 2½ cups)**

handful of fresh nettles
handful of fresh peppermint
handful of fresh parsley
300ml (10fl oz / 1¼ cups) vegetable
glycerine

*Equipment: muslin (cheesecloth)
    or super bag; 50ml (2fl oz) glass
    bottles with pipette*

A drink inspired by the book of the same name, by my dear friend
Barbara Griggs, this is a celebration of the vibrant green plants
with which we are lucky enough to co-inhabit the earth. Barbara
has truly inspired me, and I would also urge *you* to go outside,
drop your ego and day-to-day stresses and become a bee: see
what plants draw you in. Rather than a recipe, this is a guide. If
you want to add more plants, go for it. Nature is dynamic: each
leaf tastes different, so taste, taste, taste. Green drinks can be a
challenge, so lengthen this with more fruit juice, if you like. Freeze
any leftover plant juice in ice cube trays, to use later. Be safe and
follow the guidelines on collecting herbs (see page 41).

For the drink: Rinse the herbs, pass through a masticating juicer, then
follow with 50ml (2fl oz / scant ¼ cup) of spring water. Pass the fruit
through, if using. Lengthen the drink with more spring water if necessary,
then pour into a glass. Serve, adding the drops of tincture from a pipette
at the table. Float an edible wild flower or herbs on top of the drink, if you
like, and finish with a spritz of Peppermint Hydrosol.

For the Parsley, Nettle and Peppermint Tincture: You can use dried
plants here, if you do not have fresh plants. Put them in a large saucepan
with 200ml (7fl oz / scant 1 cup) of spring water, cover and place over a
low heat. Do not boil, but bring to a gentle simmer for 3–4 minutes. Turn
off the heat, allow to cool, then decant into a blender with the glycerine.
Blend for 30 seconds, then transfer into a sealable jar. Seal, shake, then store
in a dark cupboard away from sunlight for at least 14 days. Strain through
muslin cloth (cheesecloth) or a super bag and bottle in 50ml (2fl oz) glass
dropper bottles.

Lady of the Woods

In northern folklore, the silver birch tree – *Betula pendula* – is known as 'lady of the woods'. I know why, birch has a graceful, elegant, feminine presence. It offers a precious edible nectar: its sap, a cleansing tonic with blood purifying, diuretic and cleansing qualities.

Birch tapping takes place at the beginning of spring, when the water rises from the ground into the trees. While in the trees, the water takes on its naturally occurring sugars and nutrients. Collecting birch sap is brilliant fun and produces a beautifully invigorating spring tonic. Also, if you leave it out for a few days, the sugars will start to ferment, leaving a delicious probiotic tree juice…

MAKES AS MUCH AS THE TREE
WILL GIVE YOU

For the drink
1 silver birch (*Betula pendula*)

Equipment: sharp knife; mallet or hammer; hand-held drill (optional, use this if you don't have a knife and mallet); stick shaved into a point; bottle; thin rope or tape

For the Nettle and Dandelion Flower Birch Water (makes as much as the sap you collected)
handful of fresh nettles
4–5 fresh dandelion flowers
fresh silver birch sap

This is a very simple method, though also effective. (You can buy more elaborate tapping kits, with taps and pipes that will yield more sap.) Select a tree you like the look of (a healthy-looking tree; you'll know), making sure to ask permission from the tree before tapping (see page 41). At 60–90cm (24–36in) from the ground, take the knife and make an incision at a sharp upward angle into the tree, then give the base of the knife a gentle hit with the mallet or hammer so that the blade drives in 2–3 cm (¾–1¼in). (If using a hand-held drill, using a small drill bit, drill a hole at a sharp upward angle 2–3cm / ¾–1¼in deep.)

If the sap is rising, it should trickle out almost immediately. If there is no sign of it, thank the tree and return a little later. If the sap is running, take the shaved stick, place it in the incision you have just made and gently push or hammer it in at the same upward angle. The sap should run down the stick and drip from the end. Place the bottle around the end of the stick and hold it in place with rope or tape. During the main season the container will fill very quickly, sometimes in 15–30 minutes, so keep an eye on it. Once the container is full, seal and refrigerate as quickly as possible. The sap is best enjoyed immediately, or within 1 week.

Once you have collected the sap, remove the tap and press down hard around the incision; the sap will collect there and naturally form a plug. Thank the tree for its generous gifts.

You can also flavour the sap with different herbs: look at what plants are growing around the birch; herbs tend to flourish around birch trees.

For the Nettle and Dandelion Flower Birch Water: Place the nettles and dandelions in a glass jug (pitcher) or decanter, pour over the fresh birch sap and leave to infuse for 1–2 hours. The natural sugars in the sap will help to draw out the flavours and constituents from the herbs. Strain off the herbs, bottle and refrigerate the liquid and serve chilled.

The Buck's Horn Fizz

Buck Horn is another name for *Plantain coronopus*, as the older leaves are reminiscent of antlers. The leaves are highly nutritious and packed full of anti-inflammatory skin-healing secondary metabolites, as well as a host of vitamins and minerals.

SERVES 1

35ml (1¼fl oz) rhubarb juice, from organic rhubarb
50ml (2fl oz / scant ¼ cup) Elderflower and Plantain Cordial (see below)
dash of lemon juice
Sparkling Elderflower, to top up (see below)
fresh elderflowers, to serve

Equipment: masticating juicer, or juice press

Pass the rhubarb through a masticating juicer or press, making sure to strain the juice. If you do not have fresh rhubarb stalks to juice, use bought pressed apple and rhubarb juice, or just apple juice. Put the rhubarb juice in an elegant small wine or flute glass with the Elderflower and Plantain Cordial and lemon juice, top with the chilled Sparkling Elderflower, then stir and serve with fresh elderflowers.

Elderflower and Plantain Cordial
(makes about 1 litre / 1¾ pints / 4 cups)

2 full handfuls of fresh elderflower (15–20 heads), or 4 heaped tbsp dried elderflowers
2 full handfuls of fresh plantain leaves, or 4 heaped tbsp dried whole plantain leaves
1 unwaxed or organic lemon, finely grated zest and juice
500g (1lb 2oz / generous 2 cups) raw honey

Boil 750ml (1¼ pints / 3¼ cups) of spring water, then pour it into a bowl over the elderflowers, plantain leaves, lemon zest and honey, stir, cover and leave to infuse overnight (longer if you can). Strain off the mixture, add the lemon juice, then stir, bottle, seal and refrigerate. This will keep in the refrigerator for a good couple of weeks.

Sparkling Elderflower
(makes 1 bottle)

good handful of fresh or dried elderflowers
1 bottle of sparkling water

Carefully add the fresh or dried elderflowers to the sparkling water. Seal the bottle, tilt it to distribute the flowers, then refrigerate. Leave to infuse for at least 1 hour, or, better, for 3–4 hours.

Queen of Hungary

Based on an old formula shrouded in mystery but used by many, this was apparently prepared for Queen Isabella of Hungary during the sixteenth century as a restorative beauty tonic, to be used internally and externally. It is thought to be the base for the first alcoholic eau de cologne. I've created a morning beauty ritual here, featuring an invigorating drink accompanied by an antioxidant botanical face mist.

SERVES 3–4

For the drink (and morning ritual)
handful of fresh lemon balm
handful of fresh mint
1 sprig of fresh rosemary
20ml (4 tsp) rose water
60ml (4 tbsp) Sage and Citrus Oxymel (see below)
spray of Botanical Face Mist (see below)

Equipment: hand towel or cotton pad

For the Sage and Citrus Oxymel (makes about 300ml / 10fl oz / 1¼ cups)
pared zest of 1 unwaxed lemon
50g (1¾oz) fresh or dried whole leaf sage, chopped
200g (7oz / scant 1 cup) raw honey
100ml (3½fl oz / 7 tbsp) cider vinegar

Equipment: muslin cloth (cheesecloth) or super bag

For the Botanical Face Mist (makes a 50ml / 2fl oz bottle)
20ml (4 tsp) Rose Hydrosol (see page 60)
10ml (2 tsp) Calendula Hydrosol (see page 60)
10ml (2 tsp) Lemon Balm Hydrosol (see page 60)
10ml (2 tsp) Rosemary Hydrosol (see page 60)

For the drink: Place the herbs in the palm of your hand and gently clap your hands together to release their aromatic oils. Place the herbs in a glass decanter or jug (pitcher), add the rose water and 700ml (1¼ pints / generous 3 cups) of spring water and stir. Keep in the refrigerator, stirring occasionally, and allow to infuse for at least 2–3 hours. Pour in the Sage and Citrus Oxymel, stir and serve in glasses accompanied by the Botanical Face Mist, a hand towel or a cotton pad.

For the Sage and Citrus Oxymel: In a jar, squeeze out the oils from the lemon zest by gently pressing between your thumb and index finger, with the outer skin of the lemon facing towards the jar. Drop the peel in the jar, add the sage, honey and vinegar, seal and place in a pot with water almost covering the jar. Warm through for 15 minutes or so over a very low heat, but do not boil. Remove the jar and shake it gently. Store in a cupboard for at least 14 days, or longer if possible, shaking occasionally. Strain off the liquid through muslin (cheesecloth) or a super bag, bottle and seal.

For the Botanical Face Mist: Decant all the hydrosols into a 50ml (2fl oz) spray or perfume bottle. Spray on your face in the morning and wipe off with a hand towel or cotton pad.

CU29

The metal of life, copper is unique in the way it converses with its environment: it lives, breathes and communicates with its immediate surroundings. Like a work of art, it will create its own patterns and images. Copper was traditionally used – and still is – for distillation, because of the unique way it communicates and adds character to a liquid or distillate, but it is also a powerful antibacterial, so it helps to avoid any mould or fungi in the distillation process.

This is a very simple recipe to celebrate all that is brilliant about this precious metal. Featuring Indian plants that have been distilled in copper, the drink is stored in copper flasks; this is based on the traditional Ayurvedic tenet of drinking water from copper. When you store water in copper for a period of time, it actively takes on some of the copper compound, which acts as an antibacterial and positively charges the water, helping to balance the three doshas: *pitta*, *vata* and *kapha* (see page 12).

MAKES 500ML (18FL OZ / GENEROUS 2 CUPS)

3g (½ tsp) fresh or dried whole leaf tulsi
15ml (1 tbsp) Cinnamon Hydrosol (see page 60)
15ml (1 tbsp) Cardamom Hydrosol (see page 60)

Equipment: copper flask, or copper wire

Put all the ingredients in a sealable copper flask with 500ml (18fl oz / generous 2 cups) of spring water, seal, agitate by shaking and leave for 12 hours. Strain off the liquid, rinse out the flask and decant the liquid back into the flask. Enjoy at room temperature or chilled, served in copper mugs.

If you do not have access to a copper flask, you can use a glass jug (pitcher) infused with a copper wire. If you do not have hydrosols, you can use dried cinnamon sticks and cardamom pods, just add 3g (½ tsp) of each.

Restorative

Goddess Tulsi

Trikatu Shot and Milk

Goddess Tulsi

A celebration of tulsi, or holy basil, a sacred plant to the Hindus in the Indian subcontinent, a symbol of spiritual purity, famous for its restorative powers and viewed as a herbal manifestation of the goddess Lakshmi, with powerful spiritual powers. The name is derived from the Sanskrit word for 'incomparable one'. I can see why, it is beautiful in taste and effect; I find it extremely nourishing for the nervous system, helping to relieve stress and uplift the mood.

This is an East-meets-West preparation, combining tulsi with classic aromatic Western herbs.

Makes about 300ml (10fl oz)

35g (1¼oz) fresh tulsi (holy basil)
15g (½oz) fresh sage
10g (¼oz) fresh peppermint
5g (1 tsp) fennel seeds
100ml (7 tbsp) distilled water
200ml (7fl oz) vegetable glycerine
1 drop each peppermint and sage
  CO2 (optional, see page 62)

*Equipment: muslin cloth or super
  bag; 50ml (2fl oz) glass bottle*

Place all the herbs in a sealable jar with the fennel seeds, water and glycerine, seal and place the jar into a pot of hot water over a low heat (50–60°C / 122–140°F) for 2 hours. If you are fortunate enough to have access to a sous-vide machine, you can seal the liquid in a bag and leave at 50°C (122°F) for 3–4 hours.

Empty the contents into a blender, add the peppermint and sage CO2, if using, then blend and fine-strain through muslin cloth (cheesecloth) or a super bag. Funnel into 50ml (2fl oz) dropper bottles. This can be enjoyed as a few drops directly on to or under the tongue, or top up 15ml (1 tbsp) of it with warm water and serve with fresh mint leaves, for a deliciously nourishing warm drink.

Trikatu Shot and Milk

Based on a 6,000 BC Ayurveda formula called Trikatu – *tri* meaning three and *katu* meaning spicy – this formula is traditionally prepared with equal proportions of ground black pepper, ginger and long pepper as a stimulating hot tonic, particularly good for the organs of digestion, the liver, spleen and pancreas. The piperine in the pepper and the gingerols in the ginger help the body to absorb the primary therapeutic constituents of turmeric, those that give its bright orange-yellow colour.

BOTH SERVE 1

For the Trikatu Shot

2.5cm (1in) fresh organic
   turmeric root
2.5cm (1in) fresh organic
   ginger root
10 drops of Trikatu Tincture
   (see below)

Equipment: masticating juicer

For the Trikatu Milk

1 Trikatu Shot (see above)
1 glass of hot dairy or dairy-free
   milk (see page 116 for inspiration)
Trikatu Tincture, to taste (optional,
   see below)

For the Trikatu Tincture
**(makes about 300ml / 10fl oz /
1¼ cups)**

20g (¾oz) fresh organic
   turmeric root
20g (¾oz) fresh organic ginger root
10g (¼oz) dried whole black
   peppercorns
5g (1 tsp) dried long pepper
150ml (5fl oz / generous ½ cup)
   distilled water
200ml (7fl oz / scant 1 cup)
   vegetable glycerine

*Equipment: muslin cloth
  (cheesecloth) or a super bag*

For the Trikatu Shot: A short, simple and invigorating shot to get things moving, particularly great if you need a little fire and a pick me up.
Juice the turmeric and ginger root through a masticating juicer, pass 25ml (1fl oz) of spring water through the juicer, pour into an elegant small glass and drop the Trikatu Tincture in. Down in one!

For the Trikatu Milk: To create a delicious, golden milk, take the Trikatu shot and whisk through your choice of hot milk. Add a few drops of the Trikatu Tincture if you prefer it a little spicier.

For the Trikatu Tincture: Blend all the ingredients for 30 seconds and decant into an airtight sealable jar. Seal, shake well, label and store for at least 14 days (preferably longer), shaking occasionally. Strain through muslin cloth (cheesecloth) or a super bag, pressing the solids so as much liquid as possible is extracted, then bottle, seal and label. It will keep for at least 6 months.

Culpeper

Nicholas Culpeper, the seventeenth-century English physician and botanist, is a true inspiration. His book, *Culpeper's Complete Herbal*, is still one of the best texts on herbal medicine. As an astrologer, Culpeper attributed each herb to a planet, pairing plants and diseases with planetary influences.

His work is littered with interesting recipes and inspirations, and he used a famous opium-infused cordial called Godfrey's cordial. I have created a contemporary version here using poppies... obviously, minus the opium.

SERVES 1

For the drink

50ml (2fl oz / scant ¼ cup) fennel
  juice from about ½ organic fennel
  bulb, plus fennel herb to serve
50ml (2fl oz / scant ¼ cup)
  cucumber juice, from about 75g
  (2¾oz) fresh organic cucumber
10ml (2 tsp) dill juice, from a large
  bunch of dill, plus fronds to serve
25ml (1fl oz) Godfrey's Cordial
  (see below)
5–6 dashes of Calendula Vinegar
  (see below)

Equipment: masticating juicer

For the Godfrey's Cordial
(makes about 300ml / 10fl oz /
1¼ cups)
2 unwaxed lemons
15g (½oz) sassafras root
15g (½oz) aniseed
10g (¼oz) caraway seeds
5g (1 tsp) dried Californian poppy
200g (7oz / 1 cup) sugar (as
  unrefined as possible)

For the Calendula Vinegar
(makes about 200ml / 7fl oz /
scant 1 cup)
40g (1½oz) dried calendula flowers
200ml (7fl oz / scant 1 cup) apple
  cider vinegar

*Equipment: muslin cloth
  (cheesecloth) or a super bag*

For the drink: Juice the fennel, cucumber and dill, pass 75ml (2½fl oz / 5 tbsp) of spring water through the juicer, then add to a glass with the Godfrey's Cordial. Stir and add ice, then garnish with fresh fennel and dill and finish with the dashes of Calendula Vinegar.

For the Godfrey's Cordial: Peel the lemons, then put the zests in a pan with all the herbs and the sugar. Muddle or press the zest, herbs and sugar together for a minute or so, then juice the lemons and stir the juice into the mixture with 100ml (3½fl oz / 7 tbsp) of spring water. Place over a medium heat and bring to a simmer, stirring. Simmer for 4–5 minutes, then remove from the heat, allow to cool, and strain through muslin (cheesecloth) or a super bag. Bottle and seal. This will keep, refrigerated, for at least 1 month.

For the Calendula Vinegar: Place both the ingredients into an airtight sealable jar, seal, gently shake, label and store for at least 14 days (preferably longer), gently shaking occasionally. Strain through muslin (cheesecloth) or a super bag, pressing the flowers to make sure as much of the vinegar as possible is strained off, then bottle, seal and label.

Conway

Named after a truly inspirational herbalist and gentleman, Mr Peter Conway. The topic of herbs that you couldn't live without would often crop up with Peter. He would say garlic was his herb, and I agree it is up there with the most diverse and therapeutically dynamic plants on the planet. So I had to come up with an interesting recipe that included garlic. This is obviously not for those who are not keen on the smell of garlic, or in fact for anyone planning a first date.

Garlic is packed with powerful antibacterial and antiviral compounds, here extracted with honey and red wine vinegar in the form of an oxymel (see page 59). It is delicious served long with sparkling water over ice, or just enjoyed directly on the tongue, particularly when you need a lift, or if you are just feeling a little under the weather.

MAKES ABOUT 600ML (1 PINT / 2½ CUPS)

4–5 garlic cloves
handful of fresh rosemary
handful of fresh thyme, plus more
    to serve (optional)
handful of fresh sage
6 bay leaves
20g (¾oz / 2½ tbsp) crushed fennel
    seeds
150g (5½oz / 1¼ cups) fresh
    organic raspberries
250g (9oz / scant 1 cup) raw honey
250ml (9fl oz / generous 1 cup)
    red wine vinegar
1 lemon, to serve

*Equipment: muslin cloth
    (cheesecloth) or a super bag*

Crush the garlic with a mortar and pestle or garlic crusher. It's very important to do this, as the antibacterial active component in garlic – allicin – only becomes active when crushed. Add the garlic to a sterilized, airtight, sealable glass jar along with the herbs, fennel seeds and raspberries. Muddle or crush the herbs and raspberries together in the jar, add the honey and vinegar and stir vigorously. Seal the jar and add to a pan of hot water. Simmer over a very low heat for 4–5 minutes. Turn off the heat, carefully remove the jar and shake vigorously. Place it back in the hot water and leave until the water has cooled down completely. Remove the jar and dry it, shake once more, then leave it in a cool dry place away from direct sunlight for at least 2 weeks, ideally more and up to 2 months if you can. Shake the jar every day if you remember; if not, just do it when you do.

Strain the mixture through muslin cloth (cheesecloth) or a super bag, then bottle, date and seal.

To serve cold, pour 25ml (1fl oz) of the mixture into a glass with ice, top up with sparkling water and finish with a squeeze of lemon juice. To serve hot, use hot water instead of sparkling water. Serve with a sprig of thyme, if you like.

To take it directly on the tongue, decant the mixture into a 50ml (2fl oz) glass bottle with pipette. Drop 10 drops directly on the tongue when required.

Digestive Nectar

A slightly tropical plant potion with hints of aromatic spice, bursting with natural enzymes and calming constituents to help nourish and strengthen digestive function and skin health. When I talk of cinnamon I mean true cinnamon, not to be confused with its relative cassia. True cinnamon is sweeter and more fragrant than cassia. I use cinnamon for its warming and digestive calming actions, and because it tastes and smells utterly delicious. Partnered with the Queen of Spices, cardamom (another useful digestive spice), and the living enzymes in fresh pineapple and coconut, this vibrant little potion will liven up your day.

SERVES 1

For the drink
¼ fresh sweet organic pineapple, or 100ml (3½fl oz / 7 tbsp) pineapple juice (not concentrate), plus a pineapple leaf to serve
3 cardamom pods
50ml (2fl oz / scant ¼ cup) strong Cinnamon and Cardamom Infusion (see below)
100ml (3½fl oz / 7 tbsp) coconut water (fresh from the coconut if possible; if not, from a carton)
dash of lime juice
cayenne pepper, to dust

Equipment: masticating juicer (optional)

Cinnamon and Cardamom Infusion
(makes 350ml / 12fl oz / 1½ cups)
2 cinnamon sticks
5g (1 tsp) cardamom pods, split

Brew a strong infusion. Break the cinnamon into smaller pieces and crack open the cardamom pods with your fingers or the back of a spoon to expose the flavoursome seeds, place both in a teapot with a lid, cover with 350ml (12fl oz / 1½ cups) of boiling water and place the lid on. Leave until the water cools. Strain off the infusion, bottle, seal and keep in the refrigerator. You can enjoy this infusion on its own; it's delicious served either warm or cold over ice.

Juice the pineapple (or use pineapple juice) and put it in a cocktail shaker or large jam jar. Crush 2 of the cardamom pods with a spoon to release the aromatic seeds, then add to the pineapple juice with the infusion, coconut water and lime juice. Fill the shaker or jar full of ice and shake hard to create a nice foam with the pineapple. Fine-strain the drink through a tea strainer into an elegant short glass and garnish with a trimmed pineapple leaf, the remaining cardamom pod and a dusting of cayenne pepper.

Barley Water

A classic water used both in Europe and Asia to cleanse the kidneys and for its diuretic actions. It's also delicious and very cooling during the warmer summer months. Fantastic in the morning and throughout the day, it is something my grandmother used to prepare for us to drink as kids in summer. Traditional barley water seems to have disappeared in Europe, but I love it and here we are going to prepare a very simple version flavoured with lemon and penny royal, a brilliant deep, medicinal-flavoured mint.

Makes about 600ml (1 pint / 2½ cups)

250g (9oz / 1¼ cups) pearl barley
juice of 1 lemon
handful of fresh or dried penny
  royal, plus more to serve
  (optional)
raw honey, to taste

Rinse the barley, then place it in a saucepan with 500ml (18fl oz / generous 2 cups) of spring water. Stir and bring to the boil, then cover and simmer for 30–45 minutes until the barley grains are soft.

Strain the barley cooking liquid over the squeezed lemon and penny royal, then leave to infuse for 30 minutes. Add another 500ml (18fl oz / generous 2 cups) of spring water and allow to cool completely. Leave in the refrigerator overnight, strain, bottle and seal, then keep in the refrigerator and enjoy within 4 days, adding honey to taste, and a sprig of penny royal, if you like.

Galene *'Tranquillity'*

A 'Galene' was a herbal remedy (with the addition of viper's flesh and beaver secretions) created by the physician Galen, who lived more than 2,000 years ago. The precursor to the Theriac (see page 138), it contained 55 components. Don't worry, we are not going to be using anywhere near that number of ingredients here, and neither will we be employing any vipers or definitely any trace of beaver secretion. But we will be using lemnian earth, a type of medicinal clay used by Galen for its healing properties and – of course – lots of wonderful plants and minerals, all based on the original Galene.

SERVES 1

For the drink
75ml (2½fl oz) Rose and Daisy
  Sherbet (see below)
7.5ml (1½ tsp) Lemnian Earth and
  Copper Compound (see below)
75ml (2½fl oz) Copper-infused
  water (see recipe method, right)
flowers and fine red clay, to serve

**For the Rose and Daisy Sherbet
(makes about 75ml / 2½fl oz)**
2 unwaxed lemons
handful of fresh or dried rose petals
10ml (2 tsp) rose water
handful of fresh daisies
80g (3oz) sugar (unrefined)

**For the Lemnian Compound
(makes about 300ml / 10fl oz)**
5g (1 tsp) dried long pepper
5g (1 tsp) dried red clay
10g (¼oz) dried Californian Poppy
10g (¼oz) cinnamon sticks
5g (1 tsp) Peru balsam
5g (1 tsp) myrrh
3g (½ tsp) black peppercorns
2g (scant ½ tsp) white peppercorns
10g (¼oz) ground ginger
200g (7oz / ¾ cup) raw honey
100ml (3½fl oz) distilled water

Equipment: muslin cloth / super bag

For the drink: Put all the ingredients in a copper cup, three-quarters fill the cup with crushed ice, then churn the ingredients through the ice. Top with more crushed ice, stir and serve with a copper straw, freshly picked flowers (I used Californian poppy) and a dust of fine red clay.

For the Rose and Daisy Sherbet: Pare the zests from the lemons, then put the zests in a container with the rose petals, rose water, daisies and sugar. Muddle or press the zest, petals, flowers and sugar together for a minute or so, then juice the lemons and stir the juice into the mixture. Seal and leave to infuse overnight, or for at least 6 hours. Stir, strain and bottle. This will keep refrigerated for at least 1 month.

For the Lemnian Compound: Add all the ingredients to a saucepan and place over a very low heat, stirring. Warm for 3–4 minutes, but do not boil, then remove from the heat and decant into a copper flask. Seal and shake, then leave to infuse for several weeks. If you are impatient, you can use it after 2 weeks, but try to leave it for longer. Strain off the liquid through muslin (cheesecloth) or a super bag, making sure to squeeze out as much as possible (you may wish to use a tincture press, see page 52), then bottle and seal.

For the Copper-infused water: Simply fill a copper flask with spring water and leave for at least 8 hours. If you do not have access to a copper flask, you can infuse a jug (pitcher) of water with a copper coil.

Avicenna

Named after the great Persian physician Avicenna, famed for his art in distilling roses, and inspired by the classic Middle Eastern *jallab* drink traditionally made with grape molasses, carob, dates and rose water. This combines classic Middle Eastern flavours to create a stimulating sweet-and-sour pick-me-up. The rose water is key, make sure it is pure rose water traditionally produced from *Rosa damascena* or *Rosa centifolia*, due to their highly aromatic nature (for good sources, see page 190).

SERVES 1

5 tsp Persian Lime and Cardamom
  Sherbet (see below)
2 tsp rose water, plus more to serve
  (optional)
5 tbsp pomegranate juice
2 tsp pomegranate molasses
splash of sparkling spring water
rose petals, to serve (optional)
pine nuts, to serve

**For the Persian Lime and
Cardamom Sherbet (makes
enough for 3 drinks)**
4 unwaxed or organic limes
1 tsp cardamom pods
handful of Persian black limes
100g (3½oz) unrefined sugar

For the drink: Place the sherbet with the rest of the ingredients into a tumbler or highball glass, add ice cubes, stir, then finish with 2 rose petals or a spray of rose water over the top, and some pine nuts.

You could infuse your ice cubes with rose water and petals too: put 1 tsp of rose water into each compartment of an ice cube tray with 1 (unsprayed) red rose petal, top up with water and freeze.

For the Persian Lime and Cardamom Sherbet: Pare the zests from the fresh limes, then put the zests in a container with the cardamom pods, Persian black limes and sugar. Press and crush the cardamom pods, black limes and zests with the sugar for a minute or so, then juice the fresh limes and stir the juice into the mixture. Seal and leave to infuse overnight, or for at least 6 hours. Stir, strain and bottle. This will keep refrigerated for at least 1 month.

Gulab Sharbat

From the Persian word *gul* meaning 'rose' and *ab* meaning 'water', or the Arabic *julab*. It relies heavily on my favourite flavour, the rose, so make sure you source a good-quality rose water (see page 190). A classic gulab would be super-sweet and feature lots of sugar. I have dialled down the sweetness and concentrated on bringing out the best from the rose for a real fragrant treat. Incidentally, to make crushed ice, take ice cubes in a tea (dish) towel and bash it on a board with a mallet or rolling pin.

SERVES 1

For the drink
10ml (2 tsp) rose water, plus more
    to serve
50ml (2fl oz / scant ¼ cup)
    Mint and Lime Sherbet
    (see below)
handful of fresh mint, plus more
    to serve
splash of sparkling water

**For the Mint and Lime Sherbet
(makes enough for 1–2 drinks)**
4 fresh unwaxed or organic limes
100g (3½oz / ½ cup) sugar
    (as unrefined as possible)
handful of fresh mint

For the drink: Put the first 3 ingredients in a rocks glass with crushed ice, churn through using a spoon, top up with sparkling water, stir again, then cap with more crushed ice. Finish with fresh mint and a spray of rose water.

For the Mint and Lime Sherbet: Pare the zest from the limes, then put the zest in a container with the sugar and mint. Press and crush the zests with the mint and sugar for a minute or so, then juice the limes and stir the juice into the mixture. Seal and leave to infuse overnight, or for at least 6 hours. Stir, strain and bottle. This will keep refrigerated for at least 1 month.

The Wise One

Wise old sage… I love it for its diverse array of health benefits, actions and dynamism in the kitchen. I love the shape of the leaves, their fine fur, the colour, the taste, the scent… everything about sage I love. I view sage as a dear old friend, almost always there for you. I use common sage here – *Salvia officinalis* – but you can use Greek sage (*Salvia triloba*), Red sage (*Salvia miltiorrhiza*) or White sage (*Salvia apiana*). This is a contemporary take on a classic sage preparation, producing a cooling, blood-cleansing formula, a sensational late-afternoon summer cooler.

SERVES 1

10g (¼oz) fresh or dried sage, plus fresh leaves to serve
1 unwaxed lemon
75ml (2½fl oz) Lemon and Sage Sherbet (see below)

Boil 500ml (18fl oz / generous 2 cups) of water. Put the sage in a teapot, then pour over the water. Infuse, with the lid on, for 30 minutes, before straining into another jug (pitcher) or decanter. Remove a piece of zest from the lemon and juice the lemon. Add the lemon juice and the Lemon and Sage Sherbet to the drink and stir until dissolved. Keep the jug (pitcher) or decanter in the refrigerator to chill.

Serve chilled in a wine glass with the twist of lemon zest and a few fresh sage leaves.

Lemon and Sage Sherbet
(makes enough for 1–2 drinks)

3 unwaxed or organic lemons
5g (1 tsp) sage
100g (3½oz / ½ cup) sugar (as unrefined as possible)

Pare the zests from the lemons, then put the zests in a container with the sage and sugar. Press the zests with the sage and sugar for a minute or so, then juice the lemons and stir the juice into the sugar mixture. Seal and leave to infuse overnight, or for at least 6 hours. Stir, strain and bottle. This will keep refrigerated for at least 1 month, to be enjoyed as above, or with still or sparkling water.

The Courageous Man

'I, borage, bring always courage,' said John Gerard in the sixteenth century about the beautiful *borago officinalis*. I love to watch bees working on the blue star-shaped flowers (borage is sometimes called starflower); these now adorn many a cocktail in bars around the world.

Borage is brilliant for its restorative powers for the heart and lungs, particularly if you've been ill, or need strength after a stressful time. Here is a delicious, crisp, cooling summer juice; drink it while you kick back in the garden, relax and watch the bees do their work.

SERVES 1

For the drink
4–5 large borage leaves
100ml (3½fl oz / 7 tbsp) cucumber
  juice from an organic cucumber,
  plus a cucumber ribbon, to serve
50ml (2fl oz / scant ¼ cup) lettuce
  juice from organic lettuce
10ml (2 tsp) lemon juice
75ml (2½fl oz / 5 tbsp) Lemon
  Balm-infused Water, still or
  sparkling (see below)
35g (1¼oz / 2 heaping tbsp)
  Borage Flower-infused Honey
  (see below)
borage flowers, to serve

**For the Lemon Balm-infused
  Water (makes 500ml / 18fl oz /
  generous 2 cups)**
good handful of fresh lemon balm,
  or 2 tsp dried whole leaf
  lemon balm

**For the Borage Flower-
  infused Honey (makes 350g /
  12oz / 1½ cups)**
2 good handfuls of borage flowers
350g (12oz / 1½ cups) raw honey

For the drink: Pass the borage leaves through a masticating juicer with the cucumber, lettuce, lemon and a splash of the Lemon Balm-infused Water. Stir in the Borage Flower-infused Honey, add ice, top up with Lemon Balm-infused Water and serve with some fresh borage flowers and a cucumber ribbon.

For the Lemon Balm-infused Water: Take the fresh or dried lemon balm, clap in your hands to stimulate the release of some of its volatile oils, place in a jug (pitcher) or decanter, pour over 500ml (18fl oz / generous 2 cups) of spring water, stir and leave (in the sun, if there is any!) to infuse for at least 2 hours. This is delicious on its own, or in the above recipe. It's also great with sparkling water, just cram as many fresh lemon balm leaves as you can into a bottle of sparkling water, seal, gently turn upside down, then refrigerate.

For the Borage Flower-infused Honey: Place the borage flowers in a jar with the honey, place in a saucepan with warm water and heat for 2–3 minutes, but do not boil. Remove from the heat, agitate by shaking and store in a cupboard away from sunlight for at least 14 days (longer if possible, I recommend at least 1 month). Strain off the flowers if required (I just leave them in) and enjoy. If you do not have fresh borage flowers, dried borage leaf is fine, use 3–4 tsp dried whole leaf borage.

Vedic Tonic Water

A naturally sparkling Indian-inspired tonic water, gently fermented to create natural CO_2.

As with the Dandelion and Burdock (see page 162), you will need to make a soda starter, but this time using fresh turmeric root alongside the ginger. This vibrant sparkling potion is great served in a glass, then finished with a few dashes of The King of Bitters (see page 152).

MAKES 2 LITRES (3½ PINTS)

For the Turmeric and Ginger Soda Starter (makes enough for 3–4 batches)

50g (1¾oz) fresh organic turmeric root

50g (1¾oz) fresh organic ginger root

100g (3½oz / ½ cup) sugar (as unrefined as possible)

Equipment: muslin cloth (cheesecloth); elastic band

For the drink

8–10cm (3¼–4in) fresh organic ginger root

10–12cm (4–4½in) fresh organic turmeric root

125g (4½oz / ½ cup) sugar (as unrefined as possible)

150ml (5fl oz / generous ½ cup) Turmeric and Ginger Soda Starter (see above)

slice of unwaxed lemon, to serve

10–15 drops of King of Bitters (see page 152)

Equipment: muslin cloth (cheesecloth)

For the Turmeric and Ginger Soda Starter: Slice or grate around 2.5cm (1in) fresh turmeric and 1cm (½in) ginger, with the skins on, into a sterilized glass jar (see page 40), add 1 heaped tablespoon of the sugar and 500ml (18fl oz / generous 2 cups) of spring water and stir until the sugar is mostly dissolved.

Cover the jar with muslin cloth (cheesecloth) and an elastic band so it can breathe; the fermentation process requires oxygen and the cloth will keep any dust and insects away. Keep in a warm dark place, away from sunlight; an airing cupboard is perfect. Each day add another 2.5cm (1in) or so each of sliced or grated turmeric and ginger and 1 tablespoon of sugar and – importantly – stir twice a day. It should start to produce CO_2 and bubble away in 3 days. Go to the cupboard and listen to your starter; if you can hear it bubbling away vigorously without stirring, then it is ready to use. You are looking at a minimum of 3 days and up to 5 days.

For the drink: Cut or grate the ginger and turmeric into small pieces, add to a pot with 1 litre (1¾ pints / 4 cups) of spring water, cover and bring to the boil, then reduce the heat to simmer the liquid gently for 10 minutes. Turn off the heat, add the sugar and stir until dissolved. Allow the mixture to cool with the lid on. Once cool, strain off the ginger and turmeric, pour into a sterilized wide-mouthed jar (see page 40), add another 1 litre (1¾ pints / 4 cups) of spring water and the starter. Stir and place a muslin cloth over the top so the mixture can breathe without dust or insects interfering.

Leave the jar in a dark warm cupboard, stirring occasionally; after a few days it should start to bubble, the length of time it takes will depend on temperature. Once you are happy with the carbonation, strain into sterilized bottles (see page 40) and leave at room temperature for 24 hours. Chill. Serve with or without ice, a slice of lemon and the King of Bitters.

Rose and Sandal Electuary

Mastic and Ginger Electuary

Energizing

Saffron Electuary

Rose and Sandal Electuary *'honey'*

An electuary was originally an ancient Greek medicine, traditionally made with honey and combinations of herbs. They were originally intended to serve as antidotes, developed by Mithridates VI, King of Pontus, who ruled at a time when poisoning was commonplace.

The use of electuarys has declined over the years. I still think they are a fantastic base to create delicious plant potions, so here are a few contemporary variations. For sources for the dried herbs used here, see page 190.

MAKES ABOUT 500ML (18FL OZ / GENEROUS 2 CUPS)

25g (1oz) cassia bark
20g (¾oz) fresh organic ginger root
5g (1 tsp) sandalwood chips (make sure it's real sandalwood from a sustainable source)
350g (12oz / 1¼ cups) raw honey
75ml (2½fl oz / 5 tbsp) rose water

Equipment: muslin cloth (cheesecloth) or a super bag

Break up the cassia bark and finely chop the ginger, put them in a saucepan, add 150ml (5fl oz / generous ½ cup) of spring water and the sandalwood chips, cover and place over a low heat. Bring to a simmer for 3–4 minutes, stirring occasionally, but do not boil. Turn off the heat, add the honey and rose water, allow to cool completely, then transfer to a sealable jar. Seal, agitate by shaking and store in a cupboard away from sunlight for at least 14 days (longer if possible, I recommend at least 1 month but, if you can hold out, go for 6 months). Strain through muslin cloth (cheesecloth) or a super bag, bottle and seal.

If you have access to a water bath or sous-vide machine, place all the ingredients in a bag and warm on maximum temperature overnight. Leave in the bag to cool, before decanting into a sealable jar.

This is delicious as a few drops dropped directly on the tongue, or 10–15ml (2–3 tsp) served with warm water or your favourite herbal infusion is fantastic.

Mastic and Ginger Electuary *'sugar'*

MAKES ABOUT 250ML (9FL OZ / GENEROUS 1 CUP)

10g (¼oz) mastic resin
25g (1oz) cinnamon sticks
15g (½oz) fennel seeds
20g (¾oz) dried liquorice root
20g (¾oz) fresh organic ginger root, finely chopped
300g (10½oz / 1½ cups) sugar (as unrefined as possible)

Equipment: muslin cloth (cheesecloth) or a super bag

In a mortar and pestle or a coffee grinder, grind the mastic, cinnamon, fennel and liquorice. Tip these into a large bowl with the fresh ginger root and sugar. Press all the ingredients into the sugar with a spoon. Cover and leave overnight, or for a few hours.

Add to a saucepan with 250ml (9fl oz / generous 1 cup) of spring water, cover, place over a low heat and bring to a simmer for 4–5 minutes, but do not boil. Take off the heat but do not remove the lid until the mixture is cool. Strain off the mixture through muslin (cheesecloth) or a super bag, bottle and seal. This keeps in a dark cupboard for at least 3 months.

Simply serve this as a cordial, with 20ml (4 tsp) topped with a little warm water, or else serve 10–15ml (2–3 tsp) in hot water, or peppermint tea, to create a delicious digestive infusion.

Saffron Electuary

MAKES ABOUT 700ML (1¼ PINTS / GENEROUS 3 CUPS)

2 pinches of saffron threads
20g (¾oz) fresh organic ginger root
15g (½oz) cinnamon sticks
10g (¼oz) mastic resin
50g (1¾oz / ¼ cup) dried apricots
500g (1lb 2oz / 1¾ cups) raw honey

Equipment: muslin cloth (cheesecloth) or a super bag

Put 250ml (9fl oz / generous 1 cup) of spring water into a large saucepan, add all the other ingredients apart from the honey, cover and place over a low heat. Stirring occasionally, bring to a gentle simmer for 3–4 minutes, but do not boil. Turn off the heat, allow to cool, then decant into a blender with the honey. Blend for 30 seconds, then transfer to a sealable jar. Seal, agitate by shaking and store in a cupboard away from sunlight for at least 14 days (longer if possible, I recommend storing and macerating this blend for at least 1 month but, if you can hold out, go for 6 months). Strain off through muslin cloth (cheesecloth) or a super bag, bottle and seal.

If you have access to a water bath or a sous-vide machine, place all the ingredients in a bag and warm on maximum temperature overnight. Leave in the bag to cool before blending and decanting into the sealable jar.

I like to take electuaries direct, as 10–20 drops into the mouth, or in a glass of water. This saffron electuary will also invigorate freshly squeezed orange juice, just add 10ml (2 tsp) to a glass, stir and serve.

Milk of the Gods

I'm going to show you how to create rich, invigorating, nutrient-dense plant milks using nuts, seeds, herbs and spices, to give you the power of a god. These nut milks are excellent bases for your favourite invigorating plant or mushroom powders, such as Ashwagandha, or my favourite Lion's Mane mushroom. Lion's Mane – *Herecium erinaceus* – is a fungus shaped like a brain, excellent for stimulating neuron growth and for cognitive function. It tastes great, too; a teaspoon added to this recipe makes for a delicious 'brain milk'. The nuts can be swapped out for other nuts and seeds, for example cashew or pistachio, or even add a handful of sunflower seeds, so do experiment.

This luxurious milk is delicious served hot or cold, with a grating of cinnamon.

MAKES ABOUT 800ML (1½ PINTS / 3½ CUPS)

200g (7oz / 1½ cups) raw almonds
2 pinches of ground cinnamon
½ vanilla pod
3 pinches of sea salt, or to taste
5 dates (Medjool are good as you want a soft, sweet date), pitted

Equipment: muslin cloth (cheesecloth) or super bag (optional)

Cover the almonds with water and soak overnight, or for at least 6 hours. Place in a blender with the other ingredients, pour in 750ml (1¼ pints / 3¼ cups) of spring water and blend for 1 minute. I prefer not to strain the milk, as I like to eat all the protein from the nuts, but if you prefer a smooth milk, then do strain it through muslin cloth (cheesecloth) or a super bag.

Either way, taste and add extra salt if required. Place in a sealable jug (pitcher) or decanter. If refrigerated, the milk will keep for 3 days.

Ixcacao Milk

Named after the Mayan Goddess of cacao, this plant milk is packed full of nutritious nuts and seeds, stimulating cacao and the ancient Andean aphrodisiac and stimulant, maca. Maca root – *Lepidium meyenii* – used here to perk up proceedings, is famed for its bedroom-enhancing activity. It also tastes delicious when paired with chocolate!

Although Ixcacao is great served hot or cold, it's very good drunk warm in the evening, especially when it's shared with a loved one.

MAKES ABOUT 800ML (1½ PINTS / 3½ CUPS)

150g (5½oz / 1¼ cups) raw cashew nuts
50g (1¾oz / scant ½ cup) hemp seeds
1 tsp maca powder
½ vanilla pod (bean)
2 heaped tsp cacao powder
2 heaped tsp raw honey
pinch of cayenne pepper
3 pinches of sea salt, or to taste

Equipment: muslin cloth (cheesecloth) or a super bag (optional)

Cover the cashews and hemp seeds with a little water and soak overnight, or for at least 6 hours. Place in a blender with the other ingredients, pour in 750ml (1¼ pints / 3¼ cups) of spring water and blend for 1 minute.

As with Milk of the Gods (see page 116), I don't strain this, but if you want to, strain through muslin cloth (cheesecloth) or a super bag.

Either way, taste and add extra salt if required. Place in a sealable jug (pitcher) or decanter and serve chilled in summer or warm in winter. If refrigerated, the mixture will keep for 3 days.

Veda Chai

Based on an ancient Ayurvedic formula and featuring some of my favourite spices, this recipe is inspired by trips to Southern India, fuelled by the frequent road-side cups of sweet, peppery, milky, spiced masala chai. It is sweetened with jaggery, an unrefined sugar made and used in India that contains more minerals than refined sugar and is used in traditional Indian medicine. If you do not have access to jaggery, you can use unrefined sugar or a sugar alternative, or no sugar at all.

MAKES ABOUT 600ML (1 PINT / 2½ CUPS)

For the drink
5–6 tsp Spiced Tea
500ml (18fl oz / generous 2 cups) milk, dairy or dairy-free, as you prefer
jaggery, or unrefined sugar, to taste

For the Cold Infusion
4–5 tsp Spiced Tea
1 tsp jaggery, or unrefined sugar

For the Spiced Tea (makes 500g / 1lb 2oz)
40g (1½oz) cinnamon sticks
50g (1¾oz) dried ginger root
25g (1oz) dried turmeric root
20g (¾oz) dried ashwagandha root
15g (½oz) cloves
35g (1¼oz) black peppercorns
15g (½oz) long pepper
50g (1¾oz) cardamom pods
1 vanilla pod (bean)
250g (9oz / 2½ cups) good-quality loose-leaf Assam tea

For the drink: Measure out the Spiced Tea into a saucepan, add 150ml (5fl oz / generous ½ cup) of spring water and bring to the boil with the lid on. After a couple of minutes add the milk, stir and simmer with the lid on for 5–6 minutes, then add the jaggery to taste. I like it nice and sweet after dinner, or as an afternoon pick-me-up. Stir, then take it off the heat, strain off the tea and serve in small glasses with more jaggery on the side.

For the Cold Infusion: This is a delicious summer pick-me-up, either cold or at room temperature. Place the Spiced Tea in a glass jug (pitcher) with the jaggery, gently pour over a little cold or room temperature spring water to 'bloom' the tea (see page 47), leave for 30 seconds, then carefully add 500ml (18fl oz / generous 2 cups) of spring water. Stir and leave for at least a couple of hours, stirring occasionally, or up to 4–5 hours is good. You can then seal the chai in a beautiful glass bottle or decanter and keep it in the refrigerator for a few days.

For the Spiced Tea: Break down all the larger spices with a mortar and pestle or in a coffee grinder, crack open the cardamom pods to release the aromatic seeds, and split open the vanilla pod (bean) with a knife to scoop out the seeds. Then in a large bowl, mix all the spices and tea together. Once mixed, decant and store in an airtight glass container or ziplock bag, away from light, for at least 24 hours before using, shaking occasionally.

Theobroma

Named after the chocolate bean, from the evergreen tree *Theobroma cacao*. The beans (actually seeds) are collected from the trees' fruiting pods and left to ferment before being sun-dried and ground into a powder to make chocolate. Cacao contains a raft of plant secondary metabolites such as theobromine, an alkaloid that has similar actions to caffeine, with a stimulating but less intense effect on the central nervous system.

Cacao is used a great deal in traditional Central and South American cultures as a stimulant, heart tonic and diuretic. I love the bitter taste of cacao, particularly when combined with aromatic spices. Here, we make a delicious spiced chocolate blend that you can make in large batches and use as required. It's a fantastic late afternoon or evening pick-me-up, especially in winter, and can also help to spice up an evening with a loved one...

SERVES 1

For the drink

250ml (9fl oz / generous 1 cup)
  milk, or milk alternative
  (see page 116)
4 heaped tsp Theobroma Base, plus
  more to serve (optional)
raw honey or other unrefined
  sweetener, to taste (optional)

**For the Theobroma Base
(makes about 800g / 1lb 12oz)**

100g (3½oz) cinnamon sticks,
  grated (ground cinnamon will also
  work)
75g (2¾oz) cardamom pods,
  crushed
75g (2¾oz) dried whole ginger or
  ground ginger
1 vanilla pod (bean), split
10g (2 tsp) cayenne pepper
20g (¾oz) black peppercorns,
  freshly coarse-ground
500g (1lb 2oz / 5 cups) cacao
  powder

For the drink: Pour the milk into a saucepan, warm gently and add the Theobroma Base, whisking it thoroughly with the milk. Warm to a gentle simmer while whisking, but do not boil, for a good 4–5 minutes, so the milk takes on the maximum flavour from the spices. Allow the mixture to cool with a lid on, warm up when required and then strain through a tea strainer into a cup and serve. This is a relatively bitter recipe (chocolate is bitter, it's not the sweet, sugary, milk-laden product that we have become accustomed to in the West), so you can add a touch of honey or your preferred sweetener. You can also finish with whipped cream and a sprinkle of your Theobroma Base.

For the Theobroma Base: With a mortar and pestle or a blender, grind all the spices to form a spice mix. Put it in a 1-litre (1¾-pint) sealable glass jar with the cacao powder, making sure the vanilla seeds are well mixed and the cardamom pods are crushed to reveal the aromatic seeds. Seal the jar and shake it. Leave for at least 24 hours before using.

Qi

Qi in Chinese medicine is the vital force that flows through the body, and this tonic is designed to promote healthy Qi. It contains schizandra berries, that have a unique salty, sour, bitter, sweet and pungent taste. As well as containing loads of antioxidants, they enhance immune and digestive function, and are linked with increased endurance and mental capacity. They taste amazing, too.

SERVES 2

For the drink
150ml (5fl oz / generous ½ cup) pressed pomegranate juice
75ml (2½fl oz / 5 tbsp) Cold Brew Green Tea (see below)
20ml (4 tsp) Rosehip and Ginger Syrup (see below)
20 drops Schizandra and Hawthorn Tincture (see below)

For the Cold Brew Green Tea (makes 500ml / 18fl oz)
10g (2 tsp) Chinese loose-leaf green tea (I use Tie Guan Yin 'Iron Goddess')

For the Rosehip and Ginger Syrup (makes 600ml / 1 pint)
200g (7oz) rosehips, crushed
200g (7oz) sugar (as unrefined as you can get), coconut sugar or stevia (check the packet for the equivalent amount of stevia)
5cm (2in) fresh organic ginger root

For the Schizandra and Hawthorn Tincture (makes about 500ml / 18fl oz)
50g (1¾oz) dried hawthorn berry
50g (1¾oz) dried schizandra powder
100ml (3½fl oz / 7 tbsp) distilled water
400ml (14fl oz / 1¾ cups) vegetable glycerine

Equipment: muslin cloth (cheesecloth) or a super bag

For the drink: Juice the pomegranate and / or pour freshly pressed pomegranate juice into a glass jug (pitcher) with the tea and syrup and stir. Serve in tea cups, adding 10 tincture drops to each cup before your guests.

For the Cold Brew Green Tea: In a glass jug, pour 500ml (18fl oz / generous 2 cups) of spring water over the tea and stir. Leave for 3–4 hours, stirring occasionally. Strain, bottle, seal and refrigerate. The leaves can be infused again, they yield slightly different flavours, which is a good thing.

For the Rosehip and Ginger Syrup: Put the rosehips in a saucepan with 500ml (18fl oz / generous 2 cups) of spring water, cover, bring to a gentle boil, then simmer for 4–5 minutes. Allow to cool, then add the sugar, stir, cover and reheat, returning to a simmer for 2–3 minutes. Cool. Juice the ginger, add the juice to the syrup, stir, strain, bottle and refrigerate.

For the Tincture: Blend the berries and schizandra with the water and half the glycerine, then add the rest of the glycerine and blend for 30 seconds. Decant into an airtight sealable jar. Seal, shake well, label and store for at least 14 days (preferably longer), shaking occasionally. Strain through muslin (cheesecloth), then bottle, seal and label. It will keep for 6 months.

Night Fever

A special potion created for those evenings when you feel that a fever may be approaching… you know the feeling. My go-to herb for fevers is yarrow, a diaphoretic (makes you sweat), great at shifting fevers. Here, I spice it up with a little cayenne for a stimulating tonic that gets things warmed up, shifted, circulated and removed from the system.

This contains a modern version of Composition Essence, a powdered herbal extract created by an eighteenth-century US herbalist called Samuel Thomson. He used it for a number of ailments and several versions became very popular in the US at this time.

Makes 500ml (18fl oz / generous 2 cups)

For the drink
5g (1 tsp) dried yarrow leaf and flower, plus more to serve
pinch of cayenne pepper
10ml (2 tsp) Composition Essence, or to taste (see below)

For the Composition Essence (makes about 200g / 7oz)
10g (2 tsp) ground cinnamon
10g (2 tsp) ground ginger
4g (1 tsp) cayenne pepper
5g (1 tsp) ground cloves
5g (1 tsp) Sichuan peppercorns
10g (2 tsp) bayberry bark
200g (7oz / ¾ cup) raw honey

For the drink: Place the yarrow and cayenne pepper in a teapot. Boil 500ml (18fl oz / generous 2 cups) of spring water, pour the freshly boiled water over, cover and leave the lid on for 5–6 minutes. Fine strain into teacups with the Composition Essence to taste, stir and serve with dried yarrow leaf and flower.

For the Composition Essence: Put all the powders, peppercorns, bark and honey into a sealable jar, seal and place the jar in a pan with warm water. Heat for 4–5 minutes, but do not boil, then remove from the heat, agitate by shaking and store in a cupboard away from sunlight, shaking daily or when you can, for at least 14 days (longer if possible, I recommend at least 1 month). Warm up the honey and strain off the herbs, then bottle and seal.

Mrs Grieve

This drink is an ode to a special lady, Sophie Emma Magdalene Grieve, known as Maud, an English herbalist who wrote the seminal texts *A Modern Herbal Vol I & II*, first published in 1931. The digital version is still one of the best online resources for the use of herbs. I wanted to create a fitting tribute to Mrs Grieve, featuring an amalgamation of some of her original recipes.

Mrs Grieve mentions a 'Marvellous Precious Water' alongside many herbal juice, conserve and syrup recipes, and this is my version.

MAKES ABOUT 2 LITRES (3½ PINTS / 8½ CUPS)

8–10cm (3¼–4in) fresh organic ginger root
8–10cm (3¼–4in) fresh organic galangal root
125g (4½oz / ½ cup) organic cane sugar (as unrefined as possible)
2g (½ tsp) cardamom pods
2g (½ tsp) cubeb berries
2g (½ tsp) cloves
2g (½ tsp) nutmeg
3g (½ tsp) dried melilot flower and leaf
150ml (5fl oz / generous ½ cup) Ginger Soda Starter (see page 162)
slice of citrus, to serve

Equipment: muslin cloth (cheesecloth)

Cut the ginger and galangal into small pieces, add to a pot with 1 litre (1¾ pints / 4 cups) of spring water, cover and bring to the boil. Simmer the liquid gently for 10 minutes, then turn off the heat, add the sugar and spices and stir until the sugar has dissolved. Allow to cool with the lid on. Once cool, strain off all the spices and pour into a sterilized wide-mouthed jar. Add another 1 litre (1¾ pints / 4 cups) of spring water and then the Ginger Soda Starter. Stir and tie a muslin cloth (cheesecloth) over the top of the jar, so the mixture can breathe without dust or insects interfering.

Leave in a dark warm cupboard, stirring occasionally. After a few days it should start to bubble; how long it will take to carbonate depends on the ambient temperature. Once you are happy with the carbonation, strain into sterilized sealable bottles and leave at room temperature for another 24 hours. Place in the refrigerator and open once it has chilled. Serve with or without ice and a slice of citrus.

Jun

Both jun and kombucha are fermented sweetened tea drinks, popular in Asia, and now commonplace in supermarkets (grocery stores) and cafés around the world. The culture that creates both is a floating cellulose network called a scoby (Symbiotic Culture Of Bacteria and Yeast), made up of thousands of different acetic acid bacterias and osmophilic yeasts that feed off the tea and ferment the sugar. Kombucha is prepared using black tea and refined sugar, whereas jun is made with green tea and unrefined honey. The history of jun is shrouded in mystery, with tales of cultures being passed down from monk to monk in monasteries in Tibet, but I think it's a breed of culture that has been developed from kombucha. Anyway, jun is, for sure, one of my favourite drinks on the planet.

The antimicrobial activity of jun and kombucha on the body is due to the presence of organic acids, particularly acetic acid, large proteins, and catechins, which help to protect the gut and improve immune function. These fermented drinks diversify our diets and our guts, which is ever more important with the bacterial 'deforestation' of our diets due to chemically enhanced farming methods.

Scoby cultures can be bought (see page 190), but the best way to start is to be given a scoby from a friend, or by someone who is brewing jun and kombucha. It makes for a wonderful if slightly odd gift.

MAKES 2 LITRES (3½ PINTS / 8½ CUPS)

30g (6 tsp) loose-leaf green tea (I use steamed Sencha, the greener the better)
160g (5¾oz / ½ cup) raw honey
1 jun culture, comprising the scoby and surrounding liquid
20g (4 tsp) mixed dried lemon balm, lavender and chamomile

Equipment: muslin cloth (cheesecloth) or super bag; elastic band

Sterilize a glass container through a dishwasher or with boiling water. Mason jars with fitted taps are perfect (see page 190). Heat 2 litres (3½ pints / 8½ cups) of spring water to around 85°C (185°F), pour over the green tea and stir (you may need to do this in two 1-litre (1¾ pint) containers, 3 tsp in each). As the brew begins to cool, stir in the honey and make sure it is dissolved. Allow to cool completely, or you may damage the jun scoby.

Fine-strain through muslin (cheesecloth) or a super bag, making sure there is no debris. Carefully place the scoby into the sterilized glass jar with its starter liquid (the liquid from the previous fermentation; you need this to kick-start the process, there should be around 150ml /5fl oz of it). Carefully pour the mixture of green tea and honey into the glass container over the scoby, tie a muslin cloth around the mouth of the container with an elastic band, but do not seal as the fermentation needs oxygen. Place in a cupboard away from the light and leave for at least 7 days. The temperature is important, if it's too cold, it may not ferment or it can be slow to ferment; if it's too hot, it can ferment too quickly and spoil. Airing cupboards are brilliant in winter, in summer an empty, quiet cupboard is great.

Although tempting, try not to agitate the mixture, leave it alone. Sure, go and have a look, but do not disturb it. After a couple of days you will notice that strands of the cellulose network start to grow and form another culture, this is perfectly normal. After 7 days, have a little taste, it should have a lovely, perfumed sweet-sour quality. The longer you leave it the sourer it will become; I often leave it for 8–10 days as I like it nice and tart.

Pour off the liquid, making sure that you leave around 150ml (5fl oz) of starter liquid on the cultures. Then repeat the process, or seal it from air to slow down and stop the fermentation process. It will keep for a couple of months sealed, but you will need to feed it a little fresh sweetened green tea every couple of weeks. As you produce more jun the culture will grow and multiply, so you can start to produce larger batches; the culture will grow to the size of the container you are producing in. Brother and sister cultures can be given to friends, or you can separate them and start multiple batches.

Now enjoy a fresh glass of your jun, as it is delicious. We are now going to flavour it. Do experiment with types of herb, fresh and dried, types of green tea, types of honey, fermentation times, secondary fermentation times… there's lots of fun to be had here with utterly delicious results.

Pour the jun into a glass container over the dried herbs, seal and leave for 24 hours; you may wish to leave it to flavour the jun for longer, so you can experiment. Strain off the flavoured mixture. And now the important part: creating great carbonation. To do this, you need to bottle-ferment the mixture for at least 2 days (longer is better if you can). Decant the mixture into sealable sterilized glass bottles (flip-top or screw-cap are great), seal and store in the same place you fermented your brew. You can leave it for longer, just be wary that if it's too warm you will accelerate the process and may experience some lively bottles; my kitchen walls are permanently stained from super-carbonated jun and kombucha.

After 2 days, place in the refrigerator. Once chilled, carefully open and enjoy. Chilling and sealing the mixture will slow down the fermentation process, although it will continue to develop slowly over time.

Dr Dee

Brain Boosters

Dr Dee

One of Elizabethan England's most intriguing characters, Mr John Dee, 1527–1608, philosopher, alchemist, astrologer, mathematician, magician and mystic, with friends in all the right places, was at the epicentre of many of the major developments of the English Renaissance. He combined a variety of different mineral and vegetable sources to create (at times poisonous) alchemical elixirs. Inspired by and calling on the spirit of John Dee, here is a brooding dark botanical elixir (it's not poisonous, I promise), popular for its colour and detoxifying properties. Persian black limes are boiled in brine, then sun-dried so they turn black. They provide a beautifully complex, aromatic tang.

Dr Dee had a magical mirror made from a volcanic glass called obsidian. He used to call his spirits into this mirror. Obsidian is traditionally used as a protective stone, warding off negative energies and radioactive smog. Here we infuse spring water with obsidian to ward off negative energy and recreate some of Dr Dee's magic.

SERVES 1

For the drink

100ml (3½fl oz) fresh grapefruit
    juice, from organic grapefruit
5ml (1 tsp) fresh ginger juice, from
    about 5cm (2in) piece of fresh
    organic root ginger
dash of fresh lime juice
75ml (2½fl oz) Obsidian-infused
    Water (see below)
pinch of sea salt
20ml (4 tsp) Dr Dee Blend (below)
pinch of charcoal powder

Equipment: masticating juicer

**For the Obsidian-infused Water
(makes 150ml / 5fl oz)**

3–4 pieces of polished obsidian

**For the Dr Dee Blend (makes
about 500ml / 18fl oz)**

2 handfuls of black limes
1 vanilla pod (bean)
4 heaped tsp charcoal powder
5g (1 tsp) propolis powder
pinch of cayenne pepper
200ml (7fl oz) distilled water
300ml (10fl oz) vegetable glycerine

*Equipment: muslin cloth
    (cheesecloth) or a super bag*

For the drink: Juice the grapefruit, ginger and lime, strain and add the Obsidian-infused Water, sea salt, Dr Dee Blend and charcoal powder. Stir. Serve in a glass with or without ice.

For the Obsidian-infused Water: Scrub the pieces of obsidian gently under running water, place in a glass jug (pitcher) or decanter, top with 150ml (5fl oz / generous ½ cup) of spring water and leave to infuse for at least 1 hour. If you can 'charge' the water from a full moon then great: leave it in a sealed container outside for the water and stones to harness the power and vibrations of the full moon, fully calling on the spirit of Dr Dee himself.

For the Dr Dee Blend: In a cauldron… no, not really, well if you have one… if not, use a large pan with a lid on the stove top.

In the pan (or cauldron) crush the black limes with a potato masher, add the split vanilla pod (bean), charcoal powder, propolis and cayenne. Add the water and glycerine and cover. Place over the lowest heat for 7–8 minutes, then turn off the heat, leaving the lid on. Allow to cool. Blend the mixture for 30 seconds then strain through muslin (cheesecloth) or a super bag. Decant into a bottle, seal and refrigerate. This keeps for at least 3 months.

Cognitive Theriac

A brilliant little travelling companion, perfect if you have work to do that requires lots of brain and memory effort. You may have an important presentation that you have to prepare for on a plane or train, or a study or dissertation to write, or an exam to prepare for, and need some brain support. If so, a few drops of this brain-boosting potion will help no end.

This is a simple preparation based on an old Theriac, a medicinal compound made up of herbs and honey, first developed by Mithridates VI, King of Pontus (120–63 BC). It contains some of my favourite herbs for mental stimulation and peripheral circulation, and I always travel with a little bottle when I am working away from home.

MAKES ABOUT 250G / 9OZ /
GENEROUS 1 CUP

15g (½oz) fresh ginkgo
15g (½oz) fresh rosemary
20g (¾oz) fresh organic ginger root
250g (9oz / scant 1 cup) raw honey

*Equipment: muslin cloth
  (cheesecloth) or super bag; 50ml
  (2fl oz) glass bottle with pipette*

Coarsely chop up the herbs and ginger, place into a sealable jar with the honey, then place the sealed jar in a water bath or in a pot with warm water at 50°C (122°F) just to help the infusion get underway. Be careful not to heat it too much, as you don't want to denature and lose the nutrient content of the honey. Warm through for 20–30 minutes, gently shake, then store in a dark cupboard. Leave for at least 14 days, but the longer the better. Strain off the honey through muslin (cheesecloth) or a super bag, decant into a 50ml (2fl oz) glass bottle with pipette and seal. I like this directly on to the tongue, or add 5ml (1 tsp) to a cup of warm water.

Mr Maidenhair

A celebration of the oldest living tree on the plant: ginkgo, the Maidenhair tree, a botanical oddity with no living relatives. Ginkgo has grown and flourished on this planet for more than 200 million years, spreading its beautiful fanned lobe-like leaves across the globe. It is beautiful throughout spring and summer but particularly spectacular in autumn (fall), when the leaves turn golden and cover the ground.

Ginkgo is used traditionally as a brain and circulatory stimulant. It is particularly useful for improving memory. In the West, we tend to use the leaves of ginkgo, while in Asia and China they use the seeds. Here we prepare a tincture with the leaves and combine this with an 'intellect'-infused honey and other circulation- and brain-stimulating herbs, to create a memory-enhancing elixir.

SERVES 1

For the drink
handful of fresh mint
10ml (2 tsp) fresh ginger juice, from
    fresh organic root ginger
20ml (4 tsp) fresh lemon juice
25g (1oz) Intellect Honey (below)
10 drops of Ginkgo Tincture
    (see below)
fresh or dried whole ginkgo leaves,
    to serve
Equipment: masticating juicer

**For the Ginkgo Tincture
(makes about 350ml / 12fl oz)**
70g (2½oz) fresh / dried ginkgo leaf
150ml (5fl oz) distilled water
200ml (7fl oz) vegetable glycerine

Equipment: muslin or a super bag

**For the Intellect Honey
(makes about 250g / 9oz)**
25g (1oz) fresh or dried gotu kola
25g (1oz) fresh or dried skullcap
250g (9oz) raw honey

Equipment: muslin or a super bag

For the drink: First decide whether you want to drink it hot or cold,

For cold: Bruise the mint leaves by clapping them in your hands, place the bruised mint into a glass jug with 150ml (5fl oz) of spring water and infuse for 1 hour. Juice the fresh ginger and lemon and place both in a glass, then stir in the honey and the mint-infused water. Top with ice, add the drops of Ginkgo Tincture and garnish with fresh or dried whole ginkgo leaves.

For hot: Juice the ginger and lemon, add them to a glass teapot or carafe with the fresh mint and honey, pour 150ml (5fl oz) of freshly boiled spring water over the top, stir and infuse with a lid on for 5–6 minutes. Strain into a teacup with the Ginkgo Tincture and garnish with fresh or dried whole ginkgo leaves.

For the Ginkgo Tincture: Place all the ingredients into a blender, blend for 30 seconds, then decant into an airtight sealable jar. Seal, shake well, label and store for at least 14 days (preferably longer), shaking occasionally. Strain through muslin (cheesecloth) or a super bag, pressing the herb to make sure as much liquid as possible is extracted, then bottle, seal and label. It will keep for at least 6 months.

For the Intellect Honey: Crush the herbs or grind them in a coffee grinder, place in a jar with the honey, then place the jar in a pan with warm water and heat for 2–3 minutes, but do not boil. Remove from the heat, agitate by shaking and store in a cupboard away from sunlight, shaking daily or when you can, for at least 14 days, or longer if possible. I recommend storing and macerating this blend for at least 1 month. Warm up the honey and strain off the herbs through muslin or a super bag, bottle and seal.

Dew of the Sea

Beautiful rosemary *Rosmarinus officinalis* derives its name from the Latin *ros*, or 'dew', and *marinus*, meaning 'sea', and is among my favourite herbs. Its use as a medicinal and culinary herb is as old as mankind. It is a brilliant companion who is there no matter where you are in the world. Rosemary, as its name suggests, loves to be near the sea and will often be found growing on the coast. It's a great peripheral circulatory stimulant, fantastic for the brain and the stimulation of hair follicles.

SERVES 1

25ml (1fl oz) fennel juice, from an organic fennel bulb
35ml (heaping 2 tbsp) Marinus Cordial (see below)
5ml (1 tsp) Rosemary Hydrosol, plus more to serve
  (see page 60)
sparkling water, to serve
dash of lime juice
rosemary and fennel tops, to serve

Equipment: masticating juicer

Juice the fresh fennel and pour into a rocks glass with the Marinus Cordial and Rosemary Hydrosol. Top with ice and sparkling water, stir, then add a squeeze of lime juice. Garnish with fresh rosemary and fennel tops and perfume with another spritz of the Rosemary Hydrosol.

Marinus Cordial
(makes about 150ml / 5fl oz/ generous ½ cup)

5 limes
2 large pinches of fennel seeds
3–4 sprigs of fresh rosemary
2 tsp kelp powder (or fresh kelp, if you have access
  to seaweed)
150g (5½oz) sugar (as unrefined as possible)
50ml (2fl oz / scant ¼ cup) spring water
2–3 pinches of sea salt

Equipment: muslin cloth (cheesecloth) or super bag

Remove the zest from 4 of the limes and juice all the limes. Put the fennel seeds in a saucepan. Crush them with your fingers, or use the back of a spoon, then add the rosemary, kelp and sugar. Add the lime juice, lime zest and water and place over a gentle heat. Bring to a simmer, stirring, for 3–4 minutes. Remove from the heat, stir in the sea salt and allow to cool. Fine strain through a muslin cloth (cheesecloth) or super bag, bottle and seal. This cordial is also fantastic simply enjoyed with a splash of still or sparkling water.

Little Dragon

This showcases one of my favourite culinary herbs, tarragon, whose name is derived from the Latin *dracunculus* meaning 'little dragon'. It has such a beautiful flavour. Here it is combined with juicy green fruits and a touch of fennel to create a mouth-watering, cooling summer spritz.

SERVES 1

For the drink
25ml (1fl oz) fresh fennel juice, from organic fennel bulb
75ml (2½fl oz / ¼ cup) fresh green melon juice, from organic green melon, plus 1 slice to serve
50ml (2fl oz / scant ¼ cup) fresh white grapefruit juice, from about ½ organic grapefruit
20ml (4 tsp) Tarragon Oxymel (see below)
about 200ml (7fl oz / scant 1 cup) Tarragon Soda (see below)
tarragon leaves, to serve

For the Tarragon Oxymel
(makes about 225g / 8oz)
50g (1¾oz) chopped fresh tarragon (30g / 1oz dried tarragon will work, but you will lose that lovely anise flavour)
150g (5½oz / ½ cup) raw honey
75ml (2½fl oz / 5 tbsp) white wine vinegar

For the Tarragon Soda
(makes 1 bottle)
handful of fresh tarragon
bottle of sparkling spring water

For the drink: Juice the fennel and fruit into a glass, add the oxymel, top with the soda and stir. Add ice. Serve with tarragon and a slice of melon.

For the Tarragon Oxymel: Place the herbs, honey and vinegar in a jar, seal and place in a pot with water almost to cover. Warm through for 15 minutes over a very low heat, but do not boil. Remove the jar and shake. Store in a cupboard for at least 14 days, or longer if possible, shaking occasionally. Strain off the plants if you wish, though I leave them in.

For the Tarragon Soda: Bruise the tarragon by clapping in your hands. Carefully open a bottle of sparkling spring water and cram the leaves into the bottle. Seal the bottle, gently turn it upside down and leave for 1 hour, longer if possible, in the refrigerator.

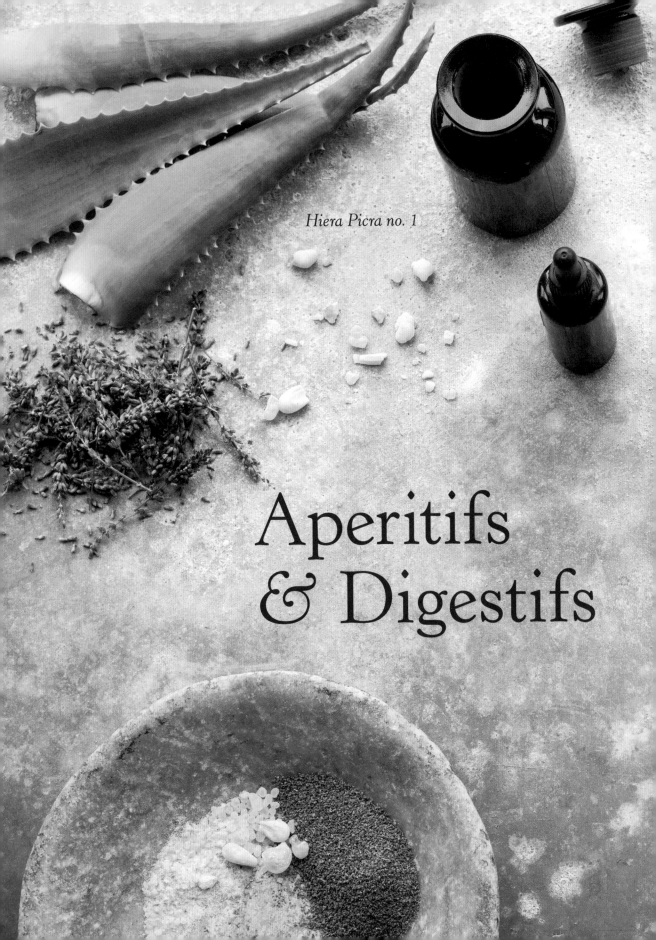

Hiera Picra no. 1

Aperitifs
& Digestifs

Hiera Picra no. 2

Hiera Picra no. 1 *'Holy Bitters'*

This is inspired by the ancient healing temples of Greece, where people came to receive treatments, usually powdered herbs, with honey to make them palatable. One formula used was the bitter Hiera Picra, for digestive, urinary and reproductive system complaints. This is my modern version. When harvesting fresh aloe, make sure it's just the inner clear gel and not the reddish-brown outer part, as this is a laxative. To extract the gel, run a knife around the periphery of a leaf to cut out the inner gel.

MAKES 400–500ML (14–18FL OZ)

200ml (7fl oz / scant 1 cup)
   distilled water
15g (½oz) frankincense
15g (½oz) mastic gum
15g (½oz) myrrh resin
1 fresh aloe leaf (inner gel only)
25g (1oz) cinnamon sticks
10g (¼oz) dried lavender
pinch of saffron threads
10g (¼oz) black peppercorns
10g (¼oz) parsley seeds
500g (1lb 2oz / 1¾ cups) raw honey

Pour the water into a large saucepan and add the frankincense, mastic and myrrh. Cover and place over a low heat, stirring occasionally. Bring to a gentle simmer, but do not boil, and simmer for 3–4 minutes. Turn off the heat, allow to cool slightly with the lid on (do not cool completely, as the resin will stick to the pan), then decant into a blender with the rest of the ingredients. Blend for 30 seconds, then transfer into a sealable jar. Seal, agitate by shaking, then store in a cupboard away from sunlight for at least 14 days (longer if possible, I recommend storing and macerating this blend for at least 1 month but, if you can hold out, go for 6 months).

If you have access to a water bath or a sous-vide machine, place all the ingredients in a bag and warm on maximum temperature overnight. Leave in the bag to cool, before blending and decanting into the sealable jar.

Take a few drops on the tongue 20 minutes before a meal, or a few drops in warm or cold water.

Hiera Picra no. 2

A second version of the Hiera Picra, traditionally formed of powdered aloe and cinnamon mixed with honey. In this recipe, I have created a versatile and delicious paste mixed with honey and coconut that can be enjoyed with your favourite plant milks (see page 116) or straight from the spoon.

MAKES 400–500ML (14–18FL OZ)

10g (¼oz) aloe powder
20g (¾oz) ground cinnamon
20g (¾oz) ground cardamom
4 pinches of saffron threads
20g (¾oz) white turmeric powder
10g (¼oz) ground nutmeg
5g (1 tsp) ground cloves
10g (¼oz) spikenard powder, or 2
   drops of spikenard oil
300g (10½oz) coconut oil
50g (1¾oz) raw honey

Place all the ingredients in a pan with the coconut oil and honey, set over a very low heat for 1–2 minutes and whisk together to mix well. Remove from the heat and decant the mixture into a glass jar, then stir and seal.

To enjoy, add 1 tbsp to your favourite nut milk (see page 116), or add some to smoothie recipes, or even enjoy it directly from the spoon.

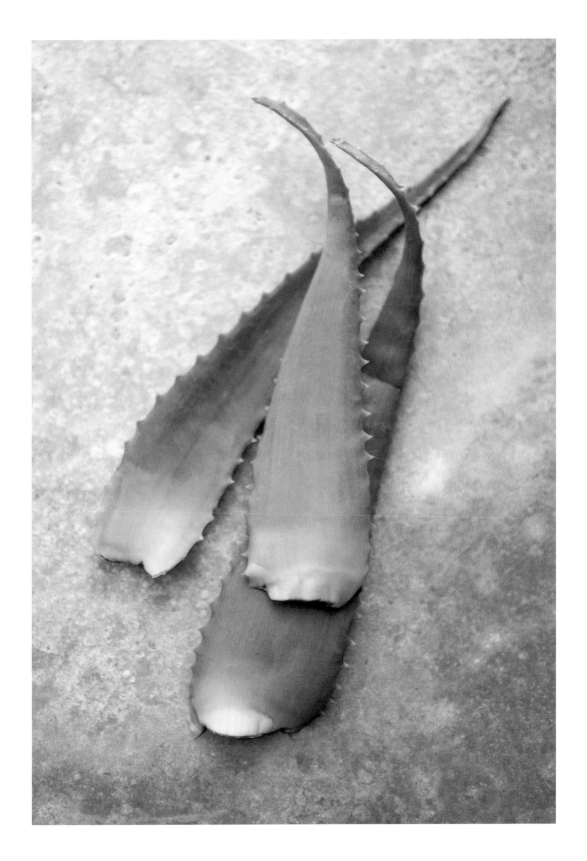

Of These Fair Isles Bitters

One of my classic bitters blends, featuring plants that grow abundantly in my homeland, this is a homage to the UK. These bitters are a gentle aromatic blend of plants and flowers featuring some of my favourite herbs. It's an excellent aperitif to help stimulate digestion, and also a great digestif to help you assimilate all that lovely food.

MAKES 400–500ML (14–18FL OZ / 1¾–GENEROUS 2 CUPS)

5g (1 tsp) dried wormwood
20g (¾oz) dried dandelion root
5g (1 tsp) dried Roman chamomile
5g (1 tsp) dried lavender
10g (¼oz) dried elderflower
10g (¼oz) dried calendula
10g (¼oz) fennel seeds
20g (¾oz) dried burdock root
5g (1 tsp) dried hops flowers
10g (¼oz) dried hawthorn berries
200ml (7fl oz / scant 1 cup) distilled water
300ml (10fl oz / 1¼ cups) vegetable glycerine

Equipment: muslin cloth (cheesecloth) or super bag; 50ml (2fl oz) glass bottle with pipette

In a coffee grinder, blender or mortar and pestle, grind all the dried ingredients into a coarse powder. Place the powder and the water into a pot with a lid on, heat through for 4–5 minutes (do not remove the lid), then allow to cool with the lid on. Once cool, pour into an airtight sealable jar with the glycerine, seal, gently shake, then label and store for at least 1 month (preferably longer), gently shaking occasionally.

Strain through muslin (cheesecloth) or a super bag, pressing the herb blend to make sure as much of the liquid is strained off as possible. Bottle in a dropper bottle, seal and label. This will keep for at least 6 months.

The King of Bitters

Named after the bitter plant *Androgaphis paniculata*, an annual herb native to India and Sri Lanka, used historically (and still, widely, today) in Ayurvedic medicine for inflammatory respiratory symptoms such as sinusitis, and for influenza. In combination with Siberian ginseng, andrographis forms part of a common off-the-shelf product called Kan Jang, sold as a cold and flu remedy for years in Scandinavia. This is my go-to combo for any sign of a cold or flu.

Andrographis is not called the king of bitters for nothing: it packs a powerful bitter kick due to a group of metabolites called andrographolides. We balance this here with classic aromatic Indian herbs, to create a wonderful pre- and post-meal invigorator.

MAKES 400–500ML (14–18FL OZ / 1¾–GENEROUS 2 CUPS)

40g (1½oz) dried andrographis
10g (¼oz) powdered Siberian
  ginseng
10g (¼oz) dried ground turmeric
10g (¼oz) cardamom pods
20g (¾oz) cinnamon sticks
5g (1 tsp) black peppercorns
30g (1oz) dried ginger root
5g (1 tsp) cloves
5 drops Cardamom CO2 extract
  (optional, see page 62)
5 drops Black Pepper CO2 extract
  (optional, see page 62)
100ml (3½fl oz / 7 tbsp) distilled
  water
500ml (18fl oz / generous 2 cups)
  vegetable glycerine

*Equipment: muslin cloth
  (cheesecloth) or super bag; 50ml
  (2fl oz) glass bottle with pipette*

In a coffee grinder, blender or mortar and pestle, grind the first 8 ingredients into a coarse powder. Place all the ingredients into an airtight sealable jar (including the CO2 extracts if you are using them). Seal, gently shake, label and store for at least 1 month (preferably longer), gently shaking occasionally. Strain through muslin (cheesecloth) or a super bag, pressing the solids to make sure as much of the liquid is strained off as possible. Bottle in a dropper bottle, seal and label. This will keep for at least 6 months.

Enjoy 10–15 drops or so with warm or cold water, before and after eating, or add to juice recipes such as Spring Tonic (see page 75).

Herball Ferment

Drinks made using lacto acid fermentation give great probiotic benefits (see page 51). These benefits for gut health mean they are perfect pre-meal digestive stimulants, particularly when created with fresh herbs. Lacto acid fermentation is a natural metabolic process; bacteria produce lots of lactic acid as an end-product of the fermentation of carbohydrates in our foods. Therefore, we use vegetables such as carrots and beetroot (beet) here, as they are high in carbohydrates. Salt is also key, as it helps to control the fermentation and prevent spoiling (lactic acid bacterias love salt and thrive in saline environments). Make sure you are using an unrefined source of salt; natural sea salt works best.

MAKES ABOUT 225ML (8FL OZ / 1 CUP)

2 large organic beetroots (beets)
6 organic carrots
1 organic fennel bulb
handful of fresh dill, plus more to
    serve
2.5cm (1in) piece of fresh ginger
    root
2 tsp sea salt

Equipment: masticating juicer

Juice the beetroots (beets), carrots, fennel, dill and ginger in a masticating juicer, strain the juice into an airtight glass container, stir in the sea salt until dissolved, seal the container and store in a cool dark cupboard for at least 1 month.

Carefully open the container and have a little sample; you may feel that you wish to ferment for longer. If you are satisfied (it should have a wonderful acidic zing in the mouth), bottle the ferment into a sealable glass bottle and place in the refrigerator (the drop in temperature will prevent further extreme fermentation).

Once chilled, decant 75ml (2½fl oz / 5 tbsp) into glasses and enjoy it 20 minutes before your meal for a tangy punch of probiotic acidity, garnished with a sprig of dill. Try and tell me you are not hungry after a little glass of this…

Sobia

On recent travels to Saudi Arabia, I came across a fermented drink prepared by fermenting grain, normally wheat, though barley is also used, then flavoured with spices such as cardamom and cinnamon. It was sad but predictable to hear that this drink's popularity was on the wane. So, it's time for a sobia revolution. I'm convinced it just needs a little contemporizing before it is reintroduced to the next generation.

When I travel, I always ask locals for old drinks recipes; this is an amalgamation of several of those and my own experiments.

MAKES ABOUT 1 LITRE (1¾ PINTS / 4 CUPS)

200g (7oz / 1½ cups) freshly milled wheat flour (good producers will label the bag with the date when it was milled)
75g (2¾oz / scant ½ cup) sugar (as unrefined as possible)
4 dates, pitted and halved
10g (¼oz) cardamom pods
pinch of saffron threads

Equipment: muslin cloth (cheesecloth) or super bag; elastic band

Put the flour in a bowl with a cup taken from 1 litre (1¾ pints / 4 cups) of spring water, then knead the mixture into dough. Add more of the water, still kneading, to create a really wet paste. Put the paste in a muslin cloth (cheesecloth) or super bag, and suspend over a sterilized glass jar or container. Squeeze the water from the paste, then gently pour the rest of the water through the flour mixture, squeezing all the water from the dough.

Once you have strained off all the water, add the sugar to the flour water and stir until dissolved, then add the dates and cover the mouth of the jar or container with muslin (cheesecloth) and an elastic band, so it is able to breathe and ferment without contamination from dust or insects. Leave the jar in a cupboard away from sunlight for 3 days, checking occasionally to make sure everything is going well (it should start to gently fizz on day 3).

Add the cardamom and saffron on the third day, stir and leave for a further 24 hours. Gently stir the mixture and strain it through muslin (cheesecloth) or a super bag into sealable glass bottles. Seal the bottles and leave at room temperature for a further 24 hours, then place in the refrigerator to slow the fermentation process and enjoy when you are ready.

As with all fermentation processes, this will be affected by different environments and temperatures, so you may wish to leave the flour and sugar mixture to ferment for longer during winter, or for a shorter time during the summer. Different parts of your home may be better for fermenting than others, so experiment with different cupboards. Also, you can add different flavours: I do a great sobia with wholemeal (wholewheat) flour and Arabic coffee, so have fun!

Mithridates and Crataeus

I couldn't write a recipe book without an ode to this original dream team of herbalism. This is based on the Mithridatum – a 2,000-year-old remedy designed to immunize against all poisons, and a 'megalium', a formula mentioned by Theophrastus in 300 BC for its anti-inflammatory properties. I've created this delicious version, which can be enjoyed pre-or post-food, with or without ice.

MAKES ABOUT 500ML (18FL OZ / GENEROUS 2 CUPS)

For the mithridatum

200g (7oz / 1¾ cup) Crataeus-
  infused Honey (see below)
100ml (3½fl oz / 7 tbsp) Cinnamon
  Hydrosol (see page 60)
50ml (2fl oz / ¼ cup) Cardamom
  Hydrosol (see page 60)
150ml (5fl oz / generous ½ cup)
  distilled water
handful of fresh mint / penny royal
bottle of sparkling spring water

For the drink: Add the honey to a measuring jug (cup) with the hydrosols and the water. Stir until mixed, then pour into an elegant decanter.

Serve after dinner from the decanter over ice, either straight or with a sparkling water infused with mint.

For Sparkling Infused Mint: Take the mint, penny royal or both, then bruise by clapping in the hand. Gently open the bottle of sparkling water, carefully place the fresh herbs inside, seal, gently turn upside down and back up again, then keep in the refrigerator to infuse for at least 1 hour.

Crataeus-infused Honey (makes 500g / 1lb 2oz / 1¾ cups)

10g (¼oz) cassia bark
15g (½oz) frankincense
5g (1 tsp) myrrh
pinch of saffron threads
5g (1 tsp) boneset
20g (¾oz) penny royal
10g (¼oz) parsley seed
15g (½oz) star anise
20g (¾oz) fresh organic ginger root
400g (14oz / 1¾ cups) raw honey
100ml (3½fl oz / 7 tbsp) distilled water

Equipment: muslin cloth (cheesecloth) or super bag

Crush all the spices using a mortar and pestle or coffee grinder, add to a sealable glass jar, cover with the honey and water, stir and seal. Place the jar in a pot with water almost to cover. Warm through for 15 minutes over a very low heat, but do not boil. Remove the jar and shake. Store in a cupboard for 14 days, longer if possible, shaking occasionally. If you have a sous-vide machine, seal the honey in a bag in it for a few hours at 45°C (113°F), then decant into a jar for 14 days. Strain through muslin or a super bag, bottle and seal.

Artemisia

In Greek mythology, Artemis is the goddess of the moon, a healing, fertilizing and nourishing protector of women and the goddess of childbirth. Silver was also attributed to Artemis; it is the colour and metal associated with the moon. The Latin name for silver, argentum, is derived from the Sanskrit word meaning 'white and shining'. The Artemisias are renowned for their beautiful silver leaves and the plants look magical when bathed in moonlight.

I love the Artemisias, an elegant, mystical and powerful family of plants. This drink is a celebration of them, a purifying, magical, silver-enriched infusion to help connect with the feminine and the moon.

MAKES 700ML (1¼ PINTS / GENEROUS 3 CUPS)

1g (¼ tsp) fresh or dried wormwood leaf, plus 1 leaf to serve

2g (½ tsp) fresh or dried mugwort

2–3g (½ tsp) fresh or dried mint (fresh is best), plus leaves to serve

2–3g (½ tsp) fresh or dried penny royal (fresh is best)

1–2g (¼–½ tsp) fresh or dried sage

2–3g (½ tsp) fresh or dried juniper berries

1 pure silver coil / wire

Place all the herbs in a glass decanter or jug (pitcher) along with the silver coil or wire, top with 700ml (1¼ pints / generous 3 cups) of room temperature spring water, then stir, stir, stir. Leave to infuse for at least 1 hour, but 2–3 hours is best. You can leave it in the refrigerator to chill, or enjoy it at room temperature. Strain off the herbs and decant into an elegant decanter with the silver coil and a fresh leaf each of wormwood and mint. Pour into glasses and enjoy.

You can make the herb blend in larger batches to enjoy at a later date; just use the above recipe as a guide and prepare what you require, then seal and store away from sunlight for up to 6 months.

Dandelion and Burdock

A contemporary version of the traditional British classic herbal drink. Here we are going to prepare a simple, natural soda with these two plants, giving them a helping hand from ginger, as ginger root contains yeasts and bacteria that are perfect for inducing natural carbonation.

MAKES ABOUT 1 LITRE (1¾ PINTS / 4 CUPS)

For the starter

100g (3½oz) fresh organic ginger root
100g (3½oz) sugar (as unrefined as possible)

Equipment: muslin cloth (cheesecloth); elastic band

For the drink

dandelion flowers (see recipe method), enough to make 750ml (1¼ pints / 3¼ cups) volume, plus more to serve (optional)
125g (4½oz / generous ½ cup) sugar (as unrefined as possible)
2 heaped tablespoons dried dandelion root (see page 190), or 3 tbsp grated fresh dandelion root
2 heaped tablespoons dried burdock root
150ml (5fl oz / generous ½ cup) starter (see above)

Equipment: muslin cloth (cheesecloth) or super bag; elastic band

For the starter: Grate or finely slice 2.5cm (1in) of the ginger – with the skin – into a sterilized glass jar, add 1 tbsp of the sugar and 500ml (18fl oz) of spring water and stir until the sugar is mostly dissolved. Cover the jar with muslin and an elastic band so it can breathe. Keep it in a warm dark place; an airing cupboard is perfect. Each day add 2.5cm (1in) grated or sliced ginger and 1 tbsp of sugar and stir twice a day. Depending on the temperature, it should start to bubble in 3–5 days. Go to the cupboard and listen; if you hear it bubbling without stirring, it is ready. Keep it going by topping up with water, ginger and sugar and stirring as before. It will be ready to use again in a couple of days. If you do not need it for a while, you can 'hibernate' it by sealing the jar and placing it in the refrigerator. Once you need her again, open her up, feed her more sugar and ginger, stir, cover with muslin (cheesecloth) and repeat; she'll be ready again in a few days.

Any natural fermentation process requires patience, you may need a slightly different environment. I have a particular kitchen cupboard that all my ferments seem to like. I've tried moving them, but they do not respond well. Try a different sugar (the less refined the better), or a different water. If it's not working for you, try a different source of ginger; organic is best as it contains the natural yeasts and bacterias needed for carbonation.

For the drink: Once your starter is bubbling away nicely, go out and pick some dandelion flowers. During spring and summer, pick the fresh flowers early in the morning on a dry, sunny day. Try to limit the amount of green sepals, as they can get a little too bitter. Half fill a 1-litre (1¾-pint) glass jar with the flowers, add the sugar and dried or fresh dandelion and burdock root, then pour freshly boiled water over the mixture, stir, stir and stir, seal the jar and let it steep overnight to create a really strong infusion.

The next day, strain it through muslin or a super bag, squeezing all the liquid from the flowers. Add to a sterilized 1-litre (1¾-pint) jar with 150ml (5fl oz) of the starter liquid, stir, then cover the mouth of the jar with muslin and an elastic band and place back into your cupboard. Stir twice daily and have a little taste occasionally, to check the balance; it should start to carbonate in 3–4 days. Once it starts to bubble, gently decant into sterilized, sealable glass bottles, seal and leave in the cupboard for another 48 hours at room temperature. Then chill; this slows the fermentation almost to a halt.

Once you are ready to enjoy, carefully open the bottles; it may be a little lively, but that's a good thing! Pour into a glass with or without ice, garnish with fresh dandelions, if you like, and enjoy.

Kyphi

Al-Kindi

Love Elixirs

Kyphi

Kyphi is one of the oldest incense recipes from ancient Egypt. Incense is still burnt in religious ceremonies but it was also commonly used internally, as a medicine. The first reference to kyphi was in the ancient Pyramid Texts, and the recipe has been developed over the years since; here is my contemporary take. For this recipe you need some time, as the resins need to infuse for as long as possible to extract their flavour and therapeutic constituents. Your patience will be rewarded.

SERVES 2

For the drink
200g (7oz / ¾ cup) Kyphi Honey
100ml (3½fl oz / 7 tbsp) Cinnamon
  Hydrosol (see page 60)
150ml (5fl oz / generous ½ cup)
  distilled water
pinch of citric acid

For the Kyphi Honey (450g/1lb)
25g (1oz) frankincense resin
15g (½oz) pine resin or dried pine
  leaves
5g (1 tsp) mastic gum
2g (½ tsp) myrrh
15g (½oz) juniper berries
30g (1oz) organic lemon grass
350g (12oz / 1 cup) raw honey
100ml (3½fl oz) distilled water

Equipment: muslin cloth / super bag

For the drink: Measure the honey into a jug (pitcher) and add the hydrosol, water and citric acid. Stir to mix, then pour into an elegant decanter.

Serve chilled, after dinner, with or without ice and (in an ideal world) with an incense burner or charcoal disk burning a mixture of cinnamon, pine, mastic and juniper berries.

For the Kyphi Honey: Crush all the spices using a mortar and pestle or coffee grinder. Put them in a sealable glass jar, cover with the honey and the distilled water, stir and seal. Place the sealed jar in a pot with water almost covering the jar. Warm through for 20–30 minutes or so over a very low heat, but do not boil. Remove the jar and agitate by shaking, then store in a cupboard for at least 1 month, longer if possible, shaking occasionally. (A 6-month extraction will produce a truly beautiful honey.) If you have a sous-vide machine, seal in a bag and place in the water bath for a few hours at around 45°C (113°F) before decanting into a jar for at least 1 month. Strain off the resins through fine muslin (cheesecloth) or a super bag, then bottle and seal.

Al-Kindi

Named after the great ninth-century Persian physician, one of the first to document in detail the techniques, methods and equipment required to distil roses. Al-Kindi was also one of the first physicians on record to prescribe rose water for ailments, including stomach disorders, liver disease and mouth ulcers. This recipe is inspired by Al-Kindi's work, but also by my travels around the Middle East, my love of the rose and of Middle Eastern flavours.

SERVES 1

For the drink

15ml (1 tbsp) pomegranate
  molasses
5ml (1 tsp) rose water, plus more
  to serve
10ml (2 tsp) Date Reduction (see
  below), or date syrup
Sparkling Hibiscus Infusion (see
  below), to top up
10 drops Rose, Oud, Cinnamon
  and Cassia Extract (see below)
agarwood chips, to serve (optional)

For the Rose, Oud, Cinnamon and Cassia Extract (makes about 250ml / 9fl oz)

2g (½ tsp) sustainable agarwood
  (oud) chips
20g (¾oz) cinnamon sticks
20g (¾oz) cassia bark
50ml (2fl oz) rose water
50ml (2fl oz) distilled water
200ml (7fl oz) vegetable glycerine

For the Date Reduction (makes about 350ml / 12fl oz)

200g (7oz) dates, Medjool or a
  similar fleshy date is good, pitted
500ml (18fl oz) spring water

For the Sparkling Hibiscus Infusion (makes 1 bottle)

1 bottle sparkling spring water
5g (1 tsp) dried hibiscus flowers

*Equipment: muslin cloth
  (cheesecloth) or super bag; 50ml
  (2fl oz) glass bottles with pipette*

For the drink: Measure out and pour the pomegranate molasses, rose water and Date Reduction into a wine glass, adding ice if you want, then stir in the glass with the Sparkling Hibiscus Infusion. Serve with dropper bottles of Rose, Oud, Cinnamon and Cassia Extract and rose water. Add drops at the table. Serve with an incense burner or charcoal disk burning oud (agarwood).

For the Rose, Oud, Cinnamon and Cassia Extract: Place all the ingredients into a blender, blend for 30 seconds, then decant into an airtight sealable jar, seal, shake well, label and store for at least 14 days (preferably longer), shaking occasionally. Strain through muslin (cheesecloth) or a super bag, pressing the herb to make sure as much of the liquid as possible is extracted, then bottle, seal and label. It will keep for at least 6 months.

For the Date Reduction: Slice the dates and place in a pan with the water. Heat and boil vigorously, stirring, to reduce the liquid by around one-third. Take off the heat and allow to cool before passing through muslin (cheesecloth) or a super bag. Bottle the liquid and seal.

For the Sparkling Hibiscus Infusion: Open the bottle of sparkling water, place the flowers inside the bottle and seal, gently turning upside down to help infuse. Leave in the refrigerator for at least 1 hour before use. There is extra here, so enjoy it either on its own or with a splash of rose water.

Love Elixir

The magic formula with which to find love has been a holy grail for thousands of years. Records of love elixirs have been traced back to ancient Egypt, Greece, Africa and South America; wherever you look throughout history and culture, in films (movies), theatre and literature, you will find elaborate recipes, potions and lotions to attract a lover. Like the search for love, this recipe does take some time, but put your heart into it and I promise you it will be rewarding.

SERVES 1

For the drink
20ml (4 tsp) rose water, plus more
  for the perfume
10ml (2 tsp) Hawthorn Tincture
120ml (4fl oz) Rose Quartz-infused
  Water, plus more for the perfume
10 drops Rose Flower Essence
  (below), more for the perfume
100ml (3½fl oz) Rose Petal and
  Raspberry Sherbet (see below)

**For the Hawthorn Tincture
  (makes 250ml / 9fl oz)**
50g (1¾oz) dried hawthorn berry /
  leaf, or fresh blossoms / leaves
50ml (2fl oz) distilled water
200ml (7fl oz) vegetable glycerine

**For the Rose Flower Essence
  (makes 1 bowl)**
1 rose bush

Equipment: muslin cloth / super bag

**Rose Quartz-infused Water
  (makes 500ml / 18fl oz)**
3–4 pieces of rose quartz

**Rose Petal and Raspberry
  Sherbet (100ml / 3½fl oz)**
2 unwaxed lemons
handful of fresh or dried rose petals
10ml (2 tsp) rose water
handful of fresh organic raspberries
80g (3oz) sugar (unrefined)

For the drink: Add everything to a chilled glass jug (pitcher) or decanter and stir. You may wish to serve this in little glasses, with rose perfume (see below). I like to decant it into little bottles with corks, seal with rose-scented red wax and label with a personalized message, as a wonderful, loving gift.

Rose perfume is simply rose water in a spray bottle, with a few drops of Rose Flower Essence and 5ml (1 tsp) of Rose Quartz-infused Water added.

For the Hawthorn Tincture: Place all the ingredients in a blender and blend for 30 seconds before decanting into an airtight sealable jar. Seal, shake well, label and store for at least 14 days (preferably longer), shaking occasionally. Strain through muslin (cheesecloth) or a super bag, pressing the herb to make sure as much of the liquid as possible is extracted, then bottle, seal and label. It will keep for at least 6 months.

For the Rose Flower Essence: When making flower essences, you are trying to capture their energy, so clear your mind, focus solely on the plant. Choose a dry, sunny day. Take a glass bowl of spring water. Place next to the roses, take a moment to be with a rose, then carefully harvest its petals and drop them on the water. Fill the surface of the bowl and leave for at least 2 hours in the sunshine, next to the plant. Carefully remove the petals, using a leaf or wooden tweezers, don't touch the water with your hands. Keep the petals for the sherbet (below). Pass the water through muslin (cheesecloth), decant into a bottle, seal and label.

For the Rose Quartz-infused Water: Cleanse the crystals by gently scrubbing them under running water, then place in the sun for a few hours. You may wish to play music to the crystals, or simply speak or pass over a positive message for them to hold. They will vibrate and share that message in the water.

Carefully add the crystals to a glass jug (pitcher), pour over 500ml (18fl oz) of spring water and leave to infuse for 2–3 hours, ideally in the sun. You may wish to cover the jug and leave it outside next to roses. Experiment and have fun.

For the Rose Petal and Raspberry Sherbet: Pare the zests from the lemons, then put the zests in a container with the rose petals, rose water, raspberries and sugar. Muddle or press the zest, petals, fruit and sugar together for a minute or so, then juice the lemons and stir the juice into the mixture. Seal and leave to infuse overnight, or for at least 6 hours. Stir, strain and bottle. This will keep refrigerated for at least 1 month.

Unconditional Love

An Indian-inspired herbal infusion featuring classic Ayurvedic herbs that help spread that unconditional love that is so needed in the world right now. It is recommended that you serve the infusion on heated rose quartz crystals, as this will continue to emanate the loving vibes. This recipe is best made in larger quantities and stored for use throughout the year, or whenever you need to spread or share more love with friends and family.

MAKES A POT TO SERVE 3–4

20g (¾oz) cinnamon sticks,
  powdered
15g (½oz) dried ginger root
5g (1 tsp) dried ashwagandha root
5g (1 tsp) dried shatavari root
15g (½oz) dried rose petals
10g (¼oz) dried rosehips
30g (1oz) dried tulsi
3–4 rough pieces of rose quartz

Mix all the dried herbs together in a large bowl, then decant into a sealable pouch or jar, being sure to store away from direct sunlight.

Cleanse the crystals, by first rinsing and gently scrubbing them under running water, then place in the sun for a few hours and whisper some love poetry to them. Place the crystals in the oven on a low heat (60–70°C / 140–158°F) for 15 minutes, or until hot. Place the crystals in teacups.

For a pot for 3–4 people, take 6 heaped tsp of the herb blend, pour over freshly boiled water, infuse with the lid on for 5–6 minutes, then fine strain and serve in cups over the warm pieces of rose quartz.

Road to Damascus

The city from which my favourite rose, *Rosa damascena*, takes its name, beautiful Damascus, famous for its rose growing and distilling, is sadly diminished. I still work with a distiller in Damascus who distils damascena rose for me. This recipe is dedicated to the beautiful people and city.

MAKES A CARAFE, OR 4–5 GLASSES

200g (7oz) raw organic pistachio
   nuts
50g (1¾oz) raw sesame seeds
20ml (4 tsp) *Rosa damascena*
   essence (see page 190)
4–5 dates, Medjool or a similar
   fleshy date, pitted, plus more
   if needed
pinch of saffron threads, plus more
   to serve
3–4 pinches of sea salt, plus more
   if needed

*Equipment: muslin cloth
   (cheesecloth) or super bag*

Place the pistachios and seeds in a large bowl. Cover with a little taken from 750ml (1¼ pints / 3¼ cups) of sparkling water, then leave for at least 4 hours or overnight in the refrigerator.

Pour the contents of the bowl into a blender with the rose essence, dates, saffron, salt and half the remaining water. Blend for a good 30 seconds to form a rich paste. Add the rest of the water, blend for a further 10 seconds, then taste to check the seasoning and sweetness, adding more salt or dates if required.

Strain through muslin cloth (cheesecloth) or a super bag. Enjoy immediately, with ice cubes and sprinkled with saffron threads, or bottle, seal and refrigerate. Refrigerated, this will keep for a maximum of 3 days.

A Modern Love Charm

Based on an old charm discussed by the great Mrs Grieve (see page 129). The traditional version was used as an anointment, and prepared on St Luke's Day with dried and powdered marigold, wormwood, marjoram and thyme, then heated and served with raw honey and vinegar. You would rub yourself down with it before going to bed, to help you find your true love.

My contemporary love charm is made by preparing an oxymel with thyme, marjoram, honey and cider vinegar. This is added to an infusion of marigold and wormwood to drink before bed, or in times when looking for love in all the right places...

SERVES 1

1–2g (¼–½ tsp) fresh or dried wormwood (go easy, it's supremely powerful and bitter, so adjust to taste)
7–8 fresh or dried marigold flowers
500ml (18fl oz / generous 2 cups) hot or cold spring water
20ml (4 tsp) Thyme and Marjoram Oxymel (see below)

If preparing cold, place the herbs in a jug or decanter, pour a little water over to bloom (see page 47), leave for 30 seconds, then top up with the rest of the water. Infuse for 2–3 hours or until the taste works for you; wormwood is really bitter. Strain off the herbs.

If preparing hot, place the herbs in a teapot or decanter, follow the above method but use hot water and only infuse for 3–4 minutes, again depending on taste.

To serve, pour the hot or cold infusion over the oxymel, stir, serve and recite, 'I will find love, I will find love...'

For the Thyme and Marjoram Oxymel (makes about 225g / 8oz)

50g (1¾oz / 1 cup) mixed chopped fresh or dried thyme and marjoram
150g (5½oz / ½ cup) raw honey
75ml (2½fl oz / 5 tbsp) apple cider vinegar

Place everything in a jar, seal and place in a pot with water almost to cover. Warm through for 15 minutes or so over a very low heat, but do not boil. Remove the jar and shake, then store in a cupboard for at least 14 days, longer if possible, shaking occasionally. Strain off the plants if you wish; I prefer to leave them in.

Oat Water

Sleep Potions

Hypnos Milk

Oat Water

A simple morning or evening skin-nourishing drink that helps to support the nervous system. It's not a coincidence in my eyes that fresh oats are almost shaped like nerves: they are so nourishing for them. Oat is a plant I gravitate towards when my nerves are frazzled.

MAKES 750ML (1¼ PINTS / 3¼ CUPS)

15g (½oz) dried oat straw
150g (5½oz) organic oats
2–3 pinches of sea salt
50g (1¾oz) raw honey

*Equipment: muslin cloth
(cheesecloth) or super bag*

Create an oat straw infusion by soaking the dried oat straw in 750ml (1¼ pints / 3¼ cups) of hot spring water, leaving it to infuse until the water cools (roughly 1 hour).

Soak the organic oats in 200ml (7fl oz / scant 1 cup) of the oat straw infusion for 30 minutes. Place in a blender with the salt, honey and the remaining straw infusion.

Blend for 30 seconds, then strain through muslin cloth (cheesecloth) or a super bag. Either drink immediately at room temperature, or bottle, seal and keep in the refrigerator, or warm through in a saucepan to enjoy hot.

Hypnos Milk

A slight variation of the above recipe, perfect in the evening, before bed or at any time when rest is required. This is a nourishing warm oat milk infused with sleep-inducing herbs, to restore and nourish the nervous system and enhance sleep.

MAKES 1 LITRE (1¾ PINTS / 3¼ CUPS)

For the drink
200g (7oz) organic oats
pinch of dried lavender flowers
pinch of dried hop flowers
pinch of sea salt
50g (1¾oz) Chamomile-infused
  Honey, or to taste (optional)
fresh lavender flowers, to serve
  (optional)

**For Chamomile-infused Honey
  (makes 250g/9oz/1 cup)**
50g (1¾oz) dried chamomile
250g (9oz / scant 1 cup) raw honey

*Equipment: muslin cloth
  (cheesecloth) or super bag*

For the drink: Cover and soak the oat flakes, lavender and hops with a little taken from 1 litre (1¾ pints / 4 cups) of spring water for 1 hour. Blend with the rest of the ingredients for 30 seconds, then pass through a muslin cloth (cheesecloth) or a super bag. Bottle the mixture and use as required, warming through over a very low heat (do not boil) and adding honey to taste and a lavender flower, if you like.

For the Chamomile-infused Honey: Place the chamomile and honey in a jar, place in a pan with warm water and heat for 2–3 minutes, do not boil. Remove from the heat, shake and store in a dark cupboard, shaking daily or when you can, for at least 14 days (longer if possible, I recommend at least 1 month). Warm up the honey and strain off the herbs, then bottle and seal.

Manzanilla

Roman chamomile (or *manzanilla*, 'little apple') is much overshadowed by its relative, *matricaria* or German chamomile, or what you get if you order chamomile tea… but not in my house. Although I like *matricaria*, particularly for children, I'm a much bigger fan of Roman chamomile: it packs more of a punch and, contrary to many studies, I find it has more of the active constituent *chameuzelene* (the blue compound that gives 'blue chamomile' its name). When picked fresh, it has a wonderful aroma of fresh green apples, but with an intriguing bitter note. It is great here, partnered with beeswax, a little pressed apple and a touch of cinnamon.

This is an excellent recipe to batch and share with friends, or make flasks to share on cold days.

MAKES 2 CUPS

For the drink
300ml (10fl oz / 1¼ cups) juice
   from organic apples
300ml (10fl oz / 1¼ cups) Roman
   Chamomile and Cinnamon
   Infusion (below)
dash of lemon juice
raw honey, to taste
3–4 dashes of Roman Chamomile
   and Beeswax Tincture (see below)
Roman chamomile flowers, to serve

Equipment: masticating juicer

For the Roman Chamomile and Cinnamon Infusion (makes 300ml / 10fl oz / 1¼ cups)
6 dried Roman chamomile flowers
1 cinnamon stick

For the Roman Chamomile and Beeswax Tincture (makes 350ml / 12fl oz
5g (1 tsp) beeswax, chopped into
   small pieces
40g (1½oz) dried Roman
   chamomile flowers
150ml (5fl oz) distilled water
200ml (7fl oz) vegetable glycerine

*Equipment: 50ml (2fl oz) glass
   bottles with pipette*

For the drink: Juice the apples and add to a pan with the Roman Chamomile and Cinnamon Infusion; gently warm but do not boil. Add the lemon juice and a little honey, stir, then fine strain into tea cups and finish with a few dashes of Roman Chamomile and Beeswax Tincture and a chamomile flower in each cup.

For the infusion: Put the dried herbs and spices in a teapot, pour over 300ml (10fl oz / 1¼ cups) of freshly boiled spring water and infuse for 5–6 minutes.

For the tincture: Place the beeswax in a sealable glass jar, seal the jar and place in hot water over a gentle heat until it melts. Remove from the water and roll the jar so the beeswax coats its insides.

Place the chamomile flowers in a teapot or separate glass jar, heat the distilled water to just under boiling and pour it over them, then seal the jar and leave until it almost cools. Add this water, its flowers and the glycerine to the beeswax-coated jar, seal and agitate by shaking. Store the jar for at least 14 days, shaking occasionally. Strain off the herbs and decant into dropper bottles.

Astral Projection

A little 'out there' potion created to help you sleep and to dream, but this will also aid you in the exploration of your dreams: astral travelling. This potion will help you to consciously be aware of your dreams and to find that dream state.

Mugwort is commonly called the dream herb. I've partnered it with the welcoming, calming influence of melissa, sleep-inducing passion flower and crystal immersions of moonstone and amethyst. This magic brew can be enjoyed directly on the tongue, dropped into a glass of water or into a cup of herbal infusion.

MAKES 50ML (2FL OZ / SCANT ¼ CUP)

For the drink
40ml (1½fl oz) Astral Tincture
  (see below)
10ml (2 tsp) Crystal Immersion
  (see below)

*Equipment: 10ml (¼fl oz) glass
bottles with pipette*

For the Astral Tincture (makes about 550ml / 19fl oz / 2½ cups)
30g (1oz) dried mugwort
30g (1oz) dried passion flower
20g (¾oz) dried melissa
250ml (9fl oz / generous 1 cup)
  distilled water
300ml (10fl oz / 1¼ cups) vegetable
  glycerine

*Equipment: muslin cloth
(cheesecloth) or super bag*

For the Crystal Immersion (makes about 100ml / 3½fl oz / 7 tbsp)
5–6 pieces of polished moonstone
  and amethyst
100ml (3½fl oz / 7 tbsp) spring
  water
10ml (2 tsp) vegetable glycerine

For the drink: Mix together both the ingredients in a small jug (pitcher), decant into dropper bottles, seal and label. Put in your bag, travel bag or by your bed.

For the Astral Tincture: Place the dried herbs in a saucepan with the distilled water (if you have time, let the herbs infuse with the water for a couple of hours before heating up). Stir, place over a very low heat with the lid on, then bring to a gentle simmer for 3–4 minutes. Turn off the heat and leave to cool with the lid on (you don't want to lose any of the aromatic compounds through evaporation). Once cool, add it all to a blender with the glycerine, blend for 30 seconds, then pour into an airtight sealable container and leave to macerate in a cupboard for at least 14 days or one full moon cycle (see page 13), gently shaking occasionally. Strain through muslin (cheesecloth) or a super bag, bottle and label.

For the Crystal Immersion: Cleanse the crystals by gently scrubbing them under running water, then place in the sun or moon for a few hours. You may wish to play some peaceful music to the crystals or simply pass over a positive message or mantra. The crystals will hold the information that you pass to them, they will vibrate and share that message in the water.

Carefully put the crystals in a glass bowl, pour over the spring water and leave to infuse for 2–3 hours, ideally in the moonlight. Carefully pour off the water, without touching it with your hands, into a bottle using a funnel. Add the glycerine and agitate by shaking.

Garden of Pleasure

Inspired by John Parkinson's 1629 book, *Paradisi In Sole Paradisus Terrestris* or 'A Garden of All Sorts of Pleasant Flowers'. Parkinson was an apothecary and distinguished botanist. His work is a joyful read on how to get the most out of gardening. This is a homage to the chapter dedicated to creating the perfect flower garden. It's a simple, fragrant cold infusion to help induce joyful dreams.

MAKES 700ML (1¼ PINTS)

2g (½ tsp) fresh or dried lavender
    flowers
5g (1 tsp) fresh or dried lime
    blossom
3g (½ tsp) marigold flowers
5g (1 tsp) dried orange peel
10ml (2 tsp) orange flower water,
    from a water distillation of
    the flowers, not from artificial
    flavourings, plus more to serve
700ml (1¼ pints) spring water

*Equipment: small perfume spray
    bottle*

Put the herbs and the flower water into a glass carafe or decanter, then gently pour over a little of the spring water just to cover the plants and allow them to bloom (see page 47). After 30 seconds or so, top with the rest of the water and stir. Leave to infuse for at least 2 hours, stirring occasionally.

Strain off the water and bottle. This will keep refrigerated for 3 days, but I like it best enjoyed in the evening at room temperature, served in a glass scented with bitter orange flower water from a spray bottle.